A Handbook of
HUMAN
RESOURCE
MANAGEMENT

D Scougl

A Handbook of
HUMAN
RESOURCE
MANAGEMENT

Michael Armstrong

**Kogan
Page**

For Peggy

First published in 1988 by
Kogan Page Ltd,
120 Pentonville Rd, London N1 9JN

Paperback edition 1990

Printed and bound in Great Britain by
Billings and Sons Limited, Worcester

A Cataloguing in Publication record for this book is available
from the British Library.

ISBN 0 7494 0144 3

Contents

1. Human Resource Management

WHAT HUMAN RESOURCE MANAGEMENT IS ABOUT

Human resource management (HRM) is an approach to the management of people, based on four fundamental principles. First, human resources are the most important assets an organization has and their effective management is the key to its success. Second, this success is most likely to be achieved if the personnel policies and procedures of the enterprise are closely linked with, and make a major contribution to, the achievement of corporate objectives and strategic plans. Third, the corporate culture and the values, organizational climate and managerial behaviour that emanate from that culture will exert a major influence on the achievement of excellence. This culture must therefore be managed, which means that organizational values may need to be changed or reinforced, and that continuous effort, starting from the top, will be required to get them accepted and acted upon. Finally, HRM is concerned with integration: getting all the members of the organization involved and working together with a sense of common purpose.

As Tom Peters wrote in *A Passion for Excellence* (William Collins, 1985):

> Trust people and treat them like adults, enthuse them by lively and imaginative leadership, develop and demonstrate an obsession for quality, make them feel they own the business, and your work force will respond with total commitment.

The same point was made much earlier by Douglas McGregor in *The Human Side of Enterprise* (McGraw-Hill, 1960) when he defined his principle of integration as: 'The creation of conditions such that the members of the organization can achieve their own goals best by directing their efforts towards the success of the enterprise.'

THE ROOTS OF HRM

The pioneers

The roots of HRM go back to the pioneering work of Peter Drucker and Douglas McGregor in the 1950s. Drucker, in *The Practice of Management* (Heinemann, 1955), virtually invented management by objectives. He wrote that: 'An effective management must direct the vision and effort of all managers towards a common goal'; this concept of visionary goal-directed leadership is fundamental to HRM.

He also castigated personnel managers in a chapter called 'Is personnel management bankrupt?' for their obsession with techniques that can become gimmicks, and for their inability or unwillingness to get really involved in the business. Drucker claimed that the personnel specialist tended to conceive his work as 'partly a file clerk's job, partly a housekeeping job, partly a social worker's job and partly fire-fighting to head off union trouble or to settle it'. He quoted with some approval a malicious saying that, 'personnel managers put together and call personnel management all those things that do not deal with the work of people and that are not management'.

Douglas McGregor advocated management by integration and self-control, partly as a form of management by objectives, but more importantly as a strategy for managing people which affects the whole business. He believed that a management philosophy needed to be built up based on attitudes and beliefs about people and the managerial role of achieving integration. He did not see this process as simply one of deploying personnel techniques, manuals and forms. A key role of the personnel function, as he saw it, was 'to devise means of getting management to examine its assumptions, to consider the consequences of its present strategy and to compare it with others'.

He, like Drucker, therefore, paved the way to the HRM philosophy that human resource policies and programmes must be built into the strategic objectives and plans of the business and must also aim to get everyone involved in the achievement of these objectives and plans.

The behavioural science movement

The behavioural science movement came into prominence in the 1960s. It was founded by writers such as Maslow, whose hierarchy of human needs placed self-fulfilment or self-actualization at the top of the pyramid, and Likert, who developed his integrating principle of supportive relationships. This stated that organization members should, in the light of their values and expectations, view their work as supportive and as contributing to the building and maintenance of their sense of personal worth and importance.

Another important figure in the behavioural science movement was Argyris, who believed that organization design should plan for integration and involvement and that individuals should feel that they have a high degree of self-control over setting their own goals and over the paths to defining those goals.

The most influential member of the behavioural science school, however, was Herzberg, who advocated job enrichment as a means of increasing organizational effectiveness, claiming that such improvements should centre on the work itself as a source of motivation – if people feel that the job is stretching them, they will be moved to perform it well.

The behavioural science movement had a somewhat idealistic flavour about it, but it did make two useful contributions to HRM. First, it underlined the importance of integration and involvement and second, it highlighted the idea that management should accept as a basic value the need consciously and continuously to improve the quality of working life as a means to obtaining increased motivation and improved results.

The organization development movement

The concepts of the behavioural scientists provided the impetus for the organizational development (OD) movement of the 60s and 70s, whose beliefs were summarized by Bennis (*Organizational Development*, Addison-Wesley, 1969) as follows:

1. A new concept of man based on increased knowledge of his complex and shifting needs which replaces an oversimplified, innocent, push-button idea of man.
2. A new concept of power, based on collaboration and reason, which replaces a model of power based on coercion and threat.
3. A new concept of organization values, based on humanistic-democratic ideas, which replaces the mechanistic value system of bureaucracy.

The OD movement advocated the implementation of programmes designed to improve the effectiveness with which an organization functions and responds to change, with particular emphasis on how people carry out their work and interact with one another. The management of change and team development are often important parts of an organization development programme.

Like the behavioural scientists they usually were, OD practitioners tended to be idealistic, but the good ones saw the organization as a whole

3

and based their plans on a systematic analysis of its circumstances and the changes and problems affecting it. This total approach to organizational behaviour exerted a strong influence on many of those who, in the late 70s and early 80s, began to concentrate on corporate culture as a central issue in the management of human resources.

The corporate culture analysts

The interest in corporate culture has derived partly from the organizational behaviour specialists but, importantly, the main thrust behind the cult of culture has come from empirical studies of the ingredients that make for corporate success.

One of the seminal works was *The Art of Japanese Management* by Richard Pascale and Anthony Athos (Simon and Schuster, 1981). This study of the secrets of Japanese business success attributed much of it to the creation of powerful organizational cultures, from which are derived shared values between management and workers which emphasize 'mutuality' – a common interest in corporate excellence.

Another influential work was *In Search of Excellence* by Peters and Waterman (Harper and Row, 1982). They found that companies whose only articulated goals were financial did not do nearly as well as companies that had broader sets of values. They quoted with approval Andrew Pettigrew, a British researcher, who saw the process of shaping culture as the prime management role. In a paper on 'The Creation of Corporate Culture' delivered in Copenhagen in 1976 he said: 'The (leader) not only creates the rational and tangible aspects of organizations, such as structure and technology, but also is the creator of ideologies, language, beliefs, rituals and myths.' Peters and Waterman found that the value sets of the excellent companies integrate the 'notions of economic health, serving customers and making meanings down the line'.

Peters and Waterman also noted that the excellent companies were people-oriented, with a wide range of 'people programmes'. Like Drucker, they warned against the 'gimmick trap' (for example, quality circles) if it is not part of an overall approach which has the absolute backing of top management and is truly representative of the corporate culture and its values.

APPLICATION OF HRM

HRM is a strategic approach to the acquisition, motivation, development and management of the organization's human resources. It is devoted to shaping an appropriate corporate culture, and introducing programmes which reflect and support the core values of the enterprise and ensure its success. HRM is pro-active rather than reactive, ie always looking forward to what needs to be done and then doing it, rather than waiting to be told what to do – about recruiting, paying or training people or dealing with employee relations problems as they arise.

The concepts of the pioneers, the behavioural scientists and the organization development specialists are built into the values underlying the programmes and will influence the techniques used in them. These techniques will include many familiar to personnel managers, such as manpower planning, selection, performance appraisal, salary administration, training and management development. These will be overlaid by special programmes designed to improve communications and increase involvement, commitment and productivity. All of them will be incorporated into a coherent approach which will link the various 'people programmes', referred to by Peters and Waterman, in a way which makes a major contribution to the achievement of the organization's objectives by being completely integrated with its strategic plans. This is the approach developed by firms such as Hewlett-Packard and IBM, described in the next chapter.

RESERVATIONS ABOUT HRM

The concept of HRM has been enthusiastically embraced by a lot of chief executives and management gurus, especially in the United States. So much so, that it has been disparaged by some people as a fad or no more than 'flavour of the month', like other managerial nostrums such as organizational development, job enrichment and similar applications of the behavioural sciences. Over-enthusiasm can kill or at least maim a fundamentally good idea.

In an article in *Personnel Management* (January 1987) Alan Fowler, while approving of much of the HRM approach, did say that the message tends to be beguilingly simple: 'Don't bother too much about the techniques or content of personnel management, it says. Just manage the context. Get out from behind your desk, bypass the hierarchy, and go and talk to people. That way you will unlock an enormous potential for improved performance.' But Fowler points out that commitment needs competence, and this includes the use of the skills of marketing, financial, production, data processing *and* personnel professionals. He also says, quite rightly, that there is a danger of implying that the HRM culture as prescribed is right for all organizations; but there is ample evidence, as will be pointed out in this book, that different situations can call for different organizations and different management styles. There is no one simple way of doing anything when dealing with organizations and people.

Some people also express reservations about the manipulative aspects of HRM. They say that, adapting the principle of 'what is good for General Motors is good for America', chief executives with a mission for HRM believe that 'what is good for the business must be good for everyone in it'. They could be right, but not always so, and all the forces of internal persuasion and propaganda may be deployed to get people to accept values with which they are not in accord and which may in any case be against their interests.

As Fowler pointed out, HRM also seems to ignore the existence of trade unions. As a system of management it starts at the top and cascades to all levels of management and staff through various processes of communication backed by specific devices such as team briefing. The emphasis is rightly on participation, but it takes two to play at that game. However hard management tries to get its message across about identification and commitment, there may still be the belief in the offices and on the shop floor that the collective interests of the work force need to be protected by trade unions or staff associations.

This could be correct: in some ways an organization is a plural society, containing many related but separate interests and objectives which must be maintained in some kind of equilibrium. Management has to work with trade unions to build harmonious relationships and to develop agreed systems of rules and procedures which will facilitate this process and resolve, with the minimum amount of damage to either party, the conflicts that will almost inevitably arise. HRM in some of its forms does not seem to recognize that this need exists.

All these are valid points, but they do not destroy the basic principles of HRM. What the reservations do tell you is that you have to be cautious about applying the HRM message too simplistically; you must avoid trying to impose an HRM type culture which is not relevant to the circumstances of the organization, or does not take sufficient account of the possibility that the values of management and workers may be too far apart to be integrated with ease.

HRM PROGRAMMES

Human resource organization

Human resource organization is concerned with achieving success by organization design and development, motivation, the application of effective leadership, and the process of getting across the message about what the enterprise is setting out to do and how it proposes to do it.

An important element will be the culture management programme which changes, shapes and reinforces the corporate culture and its values.

Human resource planning

Human resource planning sets out to define how many people the organization wants, but with particular interest in the type of people the organization needs, both now and in the future, in terms of their expertise and how they 'fit' the corporate culture.

Human resource systems

Human resource systems are the essential programmes needed to recruit, appraise, pay and look after the health, safety and well-being of the people in the organization. Two key programmes are:

1. *Performance management* which involves the appraisal of results against objectives and leads to performance improvement programmes.
2. *Reward management* which ensures that the remuneration systems adopted by the enterprise provide incentives for improved performance and rewards related to contribution and achievement.

Human resource development

Human resource development programmes meet the organization's requirement for effective and well-motivated people to achieve the results required in the short term, and to be ready for greater challenges in the future arising from innovation or growth. They will incorporate *career management* programmes which will be fully integrated with performance and reward management programmes. This will ensure that: the company has the people it needs to provide for management succession; individual managers are given the guidance and help they require to realize their potential and develop, mainly for themselves, their abilities.

Human resource relationships

Human resource relationship programmes deal with individual problems and with workers collectively as members of trade unions or staff associations. They will aim to increase co-operation and trust and to involve employees more in the company's affairs.

HUMAN RESOURCE UTILIZATION

According to Peters and Waterman, to achieve productivity through people you must 'treat them as adults, treat them with dignity and treat them with respect'. These fundamental HRM values provide the base for *productivity management programmes*, which use techniques such as method study to improve efficiency. The aim of productivity management, however, is effectiveness; this can only be achieved if its programmes are linked to other aspects of HRM and accept the HRM value sets as guidelines.

PART I

Human Resource Organization

Introduction

The fundamental objective of human resource organization is to ensure that every aspect of the organization, employment, motivation and management of people is integrated with the strategic objectives of the business and contribute to the successful achievement of those objectives.

Human resource organization, as considered in this part, provides the base and the framework for all other aspects of HRM. The base is the enterprise itself – what it is there to do and how it does it. The ingredients for success need to be identified, and these will start with the creation of appropriate strategic plans. These plans, however, and the ways in which they are achieved, will be influenced strongly by the corporate culture – the sets of assumptions, beliefs and ways of thinking, acting, and reacting which characterize the organization and strongly influence its values, how it operates and how the people in it behave. The human resource organization programme has therefore to take account of cultural issues so that the desired corporate culture can be developed or reinforced.

The framework built upon this base is the organization structure itself. However, this framework is not, as the word might imply, a static thing. It exists at a point in time to describe who does what and to define the interrelationships between the different parts of the organization, but it is subject to constant change, and around and behind the formal structure all sorts of informal processes take place. It is these that make it work.

Organizational development programmes and interventions are needed to achieve better integration, improve teamwork, manage conflict and change, and obtain commitment. These extend into how human resources can and should be motivated, bearing in mind what John Harvey-Jones said when he was chairman of ICI:

> Although many perceive its objectives as disciplined obedience to a management plan, the real purpose of management is motivation of the group to use its energy to achieve objectives. Carrots and sticks play a significant but not overriding role in generating this commitment.

The other key process in achieving success is, of course, leadership. Management, as Sir Peter Parker said at the MCE International Personnel Conference in March 1987, is 'the prime mover of enterprise', The leader has to have vision, he must be able to inspire his followers with his belief in the mission of the enterprise and, in the words of Tom Peters in *A Passion for Excellence*, he has to be an 'enthusiast, nurturer of champions, herofinder, wanderer, dramatist, coach, facilitator, builder'.

Finally, human resource organization programmes have to concern themselves with communication systems. Chief executives and managers need to share their beliefs and plans with organization members by adopting an open style of management. They must give employees the chance to get more involved in sharing *their* ideas with management. This is an important way of getting what Tom Peters described as 'turned-on people'. The organization structure itself and the proper use of information technology can facilitate good communications, but ultimately it is up to management to believe in the need to get their message across and to put their beliefs into practice by the skilful use of communication techniques and channels.

2. Achieving Success

Success is based on having the right strategic objectives and an appropriate corporate culture which embraces the values of the organization, its organizational climate and its management style. On this foundation can be built the various approaches to achieving excellence which advocate a sense of mission, the supremacy of the customer, the need for innovation, the nerve to lead with clear objectives, involvement with people and a communications policy to match. Later in this chapter summaries are given of the 'how to do it' prescriptions put forward by the leading analysts in this field, followed by a number of descriptions of 'how it was done' – case studies of successful companies and chief executives.

STRATEGIC OBJECTIVES

The organization must have a sense of purpose; a mission, if you like. In other words, there must be objectives or goals, and strategies for achieving those objectives. Only if these are defined at the highest level can the organization get what it wants done by the people it employs.

Peter Drucker was the first man to highlight the importance of corporate objectives. He wrote that: 'Objectives are needed in every area where performance and results directly and vitally affect the survival and prosperity of the business... An objective, a goal, a target serves to determine what action to take today to obtain results tomorrow... Objectives in the key areas are the "instrument panels" necessary to pilot the business enterprise. Without them, management flies by the seat of its pants – without landmarks to steer by, without maps and without having flown the route before.' (*The Practice of Management*, Heinemann, 1955.)

This is the basis of management by objectives (M by O), a technique of managing people which was first advocated by Drucker. Other people leapt on this bandwagon and produced elaborate and rigid procedures

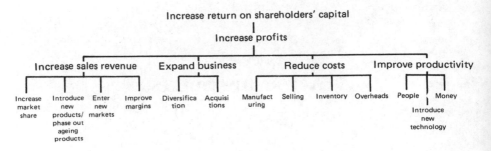

Figure 2.1 *Hierarchy of objectives*

for setting and reviewing objectives which brought the method into some disrepute. But the basic principle of M by O remains intact: people who know where they are expected to go and agree that they are going in the right direction, are more likely to get there. The organization must have a mission and the relevant part of that mission must be conveyed to each individual.

The process starts with an overriding objective, for instance, 'increase return on shareholders' capital by x%'. Beyond this point, there will be a hierarchy of objectives, as illustrated in Figure 2.1. It is this diverse range of objectives that has to be communicated to all concerned so that they know what is expected of them. The mechanisms for doing this are described in Chapters 5 to 7.

CORPORATE CULTURE

The corporate culture underlies much of the way in which things get done in the organization. It encompasses the company's goals and dominant ideologies. It can be expressed through its myths, heroes, stories, jargon, rites and rituals.

Definition

Corporate culture has been defined as the personality of an organization, but there is much more to it than that. Professor Ed Schein of the MIT, who is a leading expert on corporate culture, has defined it more formally in the *Sloan Management Review* (Winter 1984) as:

> The pattern of basic assumptions that a given group has invented, discovered or developed in learning to cope with the problems of external adaptation and integration, and that have worked well enough to be considered valid, and, therefore, to be taught to new members as the correct way to perceive, think and feel in relation to these problems.

Corporate culture can also be defined as: 'A system of shared values (what is important) and beliefs (how things work) that interact with a company's people, organizational structures and control system to produce behavioural norms (the way we do things about here).' (Dr Nicholas Georgiadis, 'Cultural Change in British Airways', MCE paper, Lisbon 1987.)

The word 'culture' has many meanings and connotations and Schein suggests that it should be reserved for the deeper level of assumptions and beliefs that are shared by members of an organization, that operate subconsciously, and that define in a basic 'taken-for-granted' fashion an organization's view of itself and its environment. In *Organizational Dynamics* (Summer 1983) he wrote that:

> Culture is not the overt behaviour or visible artifacts that one might observe if one were to visit the company. It is not even the philosophy or value system which the founder may articulate or write down in various 'charters'. Rather it is the assumptions which lie behind the values and which determine the behaviour patterns and the visible artifacts such as architecture, office layout, dress codes and so on.

How corporate culture is formed

Culture is learned. Ed Schein suggests that there are two ways in which this learning takes place. First, the trauma model, in which members of the organization learn to cope with some threat by the erection of defence mechanisms. Second, the 'positive reinforcement' model, where things which seem to work become embedded and entrenched. Learning takes place as people adapt to and cope with external pressures, and as they develop successful approaches and mechanisms to handle the technologies of their organization.

Environmental influences will make a strong impact on the corporate culture. The organization has to survive and thrive in an external environment which could be turbulent or steady, and could either drive the enterprise in certain directions whether it likes it or not, or could be managed so that the business goes where it wants to go. The type of activity the organization carries out will largely determine its technology and the way it goes about its business, and these will in turn affect the way the corporate culture develops and is manifested within the organization.

Against this background, corporate culture is created by organizational members, with the values, philosophy, beliefs, assumptions and norms of top management playing a dominant role.

The constituents of corporate culture

Corporate culture contains assumptions about the nature of the business and its markets and customers, the way in which business should be carried out, how work should be organized, the sort of people the organization needs and how they should be treated.

A corporate culture can be strong or weak, and a strong culture is not necessarily a good one – it could be the wrong culture and it could be difficult to change. A weak culture, even a practically non-existent culture, may be acceptable if the organization functions well. Within one organization there may be a dominant culture, but there will certainly be many sub-cultures in different departments or locations.

Corporate cultures are different: that at Mars is totally dissimilar to that at Cadbury's; IBM and ICL are quite unalike; no one could have anything to do with Allied Dunbar or the Prudential and not become quickly aware that they are fundamentally different. But you would be hard put to it to attribute the relative levels of success achieved by each of these pairs to particular cultural attributes.

To an extent, the interest in the concept of corporate culture has been encouraged by attempts to uncover the secrets of Japanese success. Pascale and Athos in *The Art of Japanese Management* (Simon & Schuster, 1981) emphasized the advantages of the Japanese culture in the shape of its ability to help them manage ambiguity, uncertainty and imperfection, and in its emphasis on interdependence as the most approved mode of relationship. Although there may be many good things about Japanese corporate culture which we could usefully apply in our own organizations, it is not necessarily a model which we should slavishly copy. As Pascale and Athos pointed out: 'The dozen high-performing companies identified in our study of Japanese and American firms included six that were American. The prime determinant of their success was not society or culture; it was management. United Airlines and IBM were among these firms, and in a variety of ways they outperformed their Japanese counterparts.'

How corporate culture manifests itself

Corporate culture manifests itself in organizational behaviour – how managers and individual employees or groups behave in the context of the organization. In other words, it becomes 'the way things are done around here'. The culture influences behaviour in three areas:

1. *Corporate values*: beliefs in what is best or good for the organization and what should or ought to happen. They are expressed by

reference to both ends (goals) and means (action plans for achieving goals).

2. *Organization climate*: the working atmosphere of the organization as perceived and experienced by its members. This will encompass how people feel about and react to the characteristics and quality of the corporate culture and its values.

3. *Management style*: the way in which managers behave and exercise authority. They may be autocratic or democratic, tough or easygoing, formal or informal. It also describes the way in which managers behave. Michael Maccoby in *The Gamesman* (Bantam, 1978) suggested that there are four basic types of manager:

The craftsman: an independent perfectionist whose passion is for quality and for doing things better.
The jungle fighter: a power-hungry predator who likes to be feared. Will fail where success depends on teamwork.
The company man: a courteous, loyal careerist who believes in performance and people – but wants security even more than success.
The modern gamesman: a fast-moving, flexible winner who loves change. Competes for the pleasure of the contest and for the sheer exhilaration of victory.

According to Maccoby, the ideal type is the creative gamesman – a lion with a heart who is flexible enough to behave appropriately in a variety of situations and is mentally tough but also compassionate.

The style managers adopt will be affected by the organization's culture and values. It depends to a degree on the individual's attitudes, but will also be affected by the leadership situations in which people are placed and, most importantly, by the example given by more senior managers, especially the person at the top. The chief executive by his own behaviour can exert a great influence on the management style throughout the organization.

A management style that is more likely to encourage commitment and co-operation will lean in the direction of being democratic, relaxed, friendly, informal and open. But this does not mean that it should not be tough and direct when the occasion demands it – and it should always be decisive.

CULTURE MANAGEMENT

Because corporate culture is based on taken-for-granted assumptions and beliefs about what is good and not good for the organization, it is a somewhat elusive concept. There may not be a single culture but a number of cultures spread throughout the organization; and this does not make 'managing' the culture any easier. In any case, there is no such thing as a 'good' or 'bad' culture, but only cultures which are appropriate or inappropriate. If you have an appropriate culture, its management consists of no more than maintaining the existing values, climate and management style; change is not necessary.

Corporate cultures can, however, have significant effects on behaviour. These can be fundamental if incorrect assumptions about the market and the company's position in it lead to an unsuitable strategic plan. Even when the correct strategies have been adopted, their implementation may be hindered if the wrong assumptions are made about how to sell the product or service, how to organize the people in the business, or how to manage, motivate, develop, reward and communicate with these people. Cultural change programmes may be required if the wrong assumptions have created an inappropriate culture and this is affecting performance.

Can corporate culture be managed?

Corporate culture is a key factor in achieving success but it is not easy to get at. Because it will have evolved over the years through a number of learning processes, a deeply rooted culture may be difficult to change – old habits die hard. The answer to the question, 'Can it be managed?' is, 'Yes, but with difficulty'.

However, you also have to answer the question, 'Should it be managed?' because there are a number of alternative approaches to culture management, as suggested by Howard Schwartz and Stanley Davies in *Matching corporate culture and business strategy* (MAP concept paper, 1983, Cambridge, Mass). These are:

- Ignore the culture.
- Manage round it.
- Attempt to change elements of the culture to fit the strategy.
- Change the strategy.

You can also take the culture you have got and do your best to maintain what is good about it while attempting to change counter-productive aspects of behaviour.

Alan Kennedy has said in *Corporate Cultures* that there are only five reasons to justify large-scale cultural change:

1. If your company has strong values that do not fit a changing environment.
2. If the industry is very competitive and moves with lightning speed.
3. If your company is mediocre or worse.

4. If your company is about to join the ranks of the very largest companies.
5. If your company is small but growing rapidly.

Kennedy says that if none of these reasons apply, don't do it. His analysis of ten cases of attempted cultural change indicated that it will cost between 5 and 10 per cent of what you already spend on the people whose behaviour is supposed to change and even then you are likely to get only half the improvement you want. He warns that it costs a lot (in time, effort and money) and will take a long time.

How should corporate culture be managed?

A culture management programme involves the following steps, which are described in more detail later in this section:

1. Identify basic assumptions and beliefs and challenge them if necessary.
2. Define or re-define the core values – stated or unstated.
3. Analyse the organizational climate.
4. Analyse the management style.
5. Plan and implement on the basis of steps 1 to 4 what aspects of the culture (as defined by assumptions, values, climate and management style) need to be changed and what aspects should be maintained or reinforced.

A key part is played in this process by the chief executive who, with the support of his team, achieves excellence by defining the organization's mission, getting his vision of what needs to be done across to everyone, defining and promulgating what he believes to be the right organizational values, exercising leadership in order to motivate the members of the organization, and ensuring that they are involved in and committed to achieving its objectives.

Analysing assumptions

The questions you should ask about cultural assumptions are:

● What business are we in? (discussed also in Chapter 3).
● What is the nature of our market place?
    where do we do business?
    who are our customers or clients?
● How do we do business?
    aggressive or laid-back?
    opportunistic or reactive?

dynamic or static?
emphasis on personal or professional skills?
take the competition head on or seek gaps in the market?
market or production/technology oriented?
- How should work be organized?
structured (mechanistic) or fluid (organic)?
bureaucratic or informal?
multi-level or flat structure?
- What sort of people do we need in the organization in terms of quality, expertise and professional qualifications?
- How do we treat people in the organization?
as partners or servants?
in close contact or at arm's length?
openly (trusted with information) or closed (kept in the dark)?
as able not only to accept but also to seek responsibility (Douglas McGregor's theory Y) or as requiring coercion, control, and direction and the threat of punishment to get them to put forth adequate effort toward the achievement of organizational objectives (McGregor's theory X)?
as needing the carrot more than the stick or vice versa?

The assumptions could be invalid, in which case they need to be challenged, or they could be valid and not acted upon, in which case they need to be reinforced.

Analysing values

The questions you should ask about values are:

- Are employees proud of the company and its products or services?
- Does the company truly believe in producing high quality products and providing a good service to its customers?
- Is the company innovative?
- Are managers and employees really interested in increasing productivity?
- Do managers truly believe in the importance of the people who work there? Are they committed to improving the quality of working life, providing opportunities for growth and development, giving individual attention to the needs of employees, keeping them informed on matters that affect them and involved in decision making, and maintaining a fair pay system which rewards staff according to their responsibilities and contribution?

A belief in these values and in the organization as a whole will be developed if something that is worth doing is being done well. Pride in the product and pride in the company may exist because of a long tradition of achievement and quality. But identification and loyalty are not inevitable; they have to be fostered.

Values will only be got across if they are believed in, acted upon and pursued relentlessly. The responsibility for presenting them should start at the top, but it should be shared among all managers and supervisors. You may not wish to go quite as far as the Japanese (in Japan, at 8 am every working day 87,000 Matsushita employees sing the company song and recite the company's code of values), but it has to be accepted that their belief in getting the total identification of employees with their company has paid off.

Analysing organization climate

The questions you should ask about organization climate are:

- Do people feel they are given enough responsibility?
- Do people know what is expected of them in the shape of objectives and standards of performance?
- Is there adequate feedback to people on their performance, whether it is good, bad or indifferent?
- Is there sufficient challenge in the jobs given to people and sufficient emphasis on doing a good job (eg a strong drive for professionalism among managers)?
- Are people given enough support by their managers or supervisors in the shape of guidance or help?
- Is the emphasis in the organization on hard, dedicated work, or is it fairly relaxed?
- Do people feel they are fairly rewarded for the work they do?
- Do people feel that promotion policies are fair?
- Is there an emphasis on positive rewards rather than punishments?
- Is there a lot of bureaucracy and red tape around the organization or is the approach to work reasonably flexible and informal?
- Is there an emphasis on taking calculated risks in the organization, or is playing it safe the general rule?
- Is management open about what the company is doing?
- Is there a general feeling of warmth and good fellowship in the atmosphere?
- Do managers and other employees *want* to hear different opinions?
- Is the emphasis on getting problems out into the open rather than smoothing them over or ignoring them?

- Do people feel that they belong to a worthwhile company and are valuable members of working teams?

Analysing management style

The questions you should ask about management style are:

- Does it tend to be autocratic, ie using authority to compel people to do what they are told, or democratic, ie encouraging people to participate and involve themselves in decision making?
- Does it tend to be task-centred or people-centred?
- Do managers tend to be distant and cold or approachable and friendly?
- Do managers tend to be hard or soft on people?

The culture change or reinforcement programme

The analysis of assumptions, values, climate and management style should indicate any areas where changes need to be made or the existing situation reinforced. The first thing to remember about culture change is that it can be difficult, painful and prolonged. Don't expect quick results; fundamental changes can take years – and anticipate resistance to change. Cultural assumptions and values may be deeply entrenched and people will not give them up easily. You cannot simply issue a new charter of corporate values and expect people to act on them wholeheartedly and at once. They have to be convinced that they are relevant and valid and will not adversely affect their own position in the organization.

There are two ways of tackling change. The first is to deal with the various manifestations of culture in a general way, allowing particular programmes to emerge from this process. The second is to go straight for one or more specific areas, having first defined your objectives – what change you want to bring about and why. Be general when you need to explore in greater depth what needs to be done; be specific when you are quite clear about where you are going. But don't try to do too much at once.

General approaches to cultural change

The general approaches to cultural change will examine:

Assumptions
Get people to challenge them whenever they emerge specifically in

discussions, meetings or memoranda or appear to underlie opinions expressed orally or on paper. Use the checklist given earlier in this section and re-examine them in discussion. No dramatic changes will be achieved by this means alone, but at least people will become more aware of what they have previously taken for granted and may be more willing to change their behaviour as a result of other aspects of the programme.

Values
Consciously and deliberately set out the core values of the organization and get them discussed at board level and throughout the organization. Re-state them formally on the basis of these discussions but ensure also that these values are reinforced and acted upon by other cultural change activities as described below.

Organization climate
Ask people what they think is good and bad about the climate. This can be done comprehensively by an attitude survey or by using focus groups – special semi-structured discussion groups of employees aimed at eliciting shared attitudes and beliefs about the organization.

Management style
A change in management style is best achieved by example from above, starting at the top of the organization. Management style will also be strongly influenced by re-statements and examinations of values and climate.

When managers are appraised, their management style should be a subject for discussion, and agreement should be reached between the people concerned on where changes are desirable. Appraisals should be both downwards from management to subordinate, and upwards – the subordinate should be given the chance to appraise his manager. Self-appraisal should also be encouraged.

Specific approaches to cultural change

The specific approaches you can use to achieve cultural change are:

1. *Reorganization* to facilitate integration, to create departments or jobs which are responsible for new activities or to eliminate unnecessary layers of management.
2. *Organization development* to improve the effectiveness with which an organization functions and responds to change. OD programmes, as described in Chapter 4, are concerned with achieving better co-ordination, teamwork and commitment and with the management of change and conflict.

3. *Communications* to get the message across about the values and to achieve the objectives for a communications change programme set up in Book Club Associates in 1987, which were to:
   - increase the identification of staff with the firm and therefore to enhance their commitment;
   - provide the opportunity for all levels of staff to become more involved in the firm's affairs;
   - generate ideas from staff to develop the business, improve the levels of customer service and increase productivity.
4. *Training* to help form new attitudes to such matters as customer service, quality, managing and motivating people or productivity; to increase commitment to the firm and its values; to review and challenge assumptions; and to improve skills or teach new skills.
5. *Recruitment* to set out deliberately to change the type of people recruited to fit the desired culture or to reinforce the existing culture by drawing up related job specifications and finding candidates who meet those specifications.
6. *Management by objectives* to ensure that managers know what they are expected to do.
7. *Performance management* to ensure that managers, supervisors and staff are assessed on the basis of the results they achieve and that performance improvement programmes consisting of self-development, coaching, counselling and training are used to capitalize on strengths or overcome weaknesses.
8. *Reward management* to enhance the cultural assumption that rewards should be related to achievement by introducing performance related bonus schemes and remuneration systems.

EXAMPLES OF CULTURAL CHANGE PROGRAMMES

British Airways

To quote Dr Nicholas Georgiadis, director of human resources at British Airways, speaking at the MCE conference in Lisbon in 1987: 'British Airways has changed. Five years ago it was sick. It is now much healthier. At the roots of that recovery (from losses of £111 million in 1981/82 to cumulative profits of £536 million over the last three years) is customer service.'

The dominant culture in British Airways, according to Georgiadis, had been militaristic and bureaucratic. His comment on this was that: 'You cannot determine human behaviour by referring to paragraph 3(9)x. You cannot provide quality customer service by administrative fiat. What you have to have is an empowered work force – a work force which knows it has the power to take action and that its decisions will be backed by the bosses.'

The British Airways management decided that the main area for cultural change was customer service; and that the key to successful customer service lies in ensuring that people feel good about themselves and their company. In short, customer care demands caring, skilful management to support the caring skills for which British Airways managers were 'untrained, uninformed and unrewarded'.

The culture change programme was divided into three parts:

1. *'Putting people first'*: a two-day intensive workshop aimed at all customer contact staff, encouraging them to think about the importance of customer service. The workshop looked at issues such as: the importance of helping other people give good customer service; who owns a customer's problem; and the importance of body language in all human interaction. All 40,000 employees went through this programme.
2. *'A day in the life'*: a one-day event designed to help all staff understand their mutual interdependence. Some 30,000 staff enjoyed this day.
3. *Managing people first*: a five-and-a-half-day event for managers which dealt with five themes:
   - *Urgency* which should come from the leader, not from events. This means that managers must be pro-active rather than running just to stand still as they simply react to events;
   - *Vision* which is 'having the image of the cathedral as we mix the cement'. Managers must be able to work both in the here and now, as they mix the cement, and focus on the future as they plan the cathedral;
   - *Motivation* which is management by expectation. Expect the best and catch them doing it right, because people who feel good about themselves and their manager produce good results;
   - *Trust* which gives confidence to the individual to act alone – and spirit to the group to act together – freeing people to own the problem and use their own judgement without fear;
   - above all, *responsibility* – believing that: I am in charge of my own behaviour, which means that I can change the way I do things.

In addition to these courses, a new performance appraisal scheme was introduced, based on the mentor system which focused on managerial behaviour, especially team management and the management of subordinates. Having been told how to do it in the managing people first programme, appraisal tells them how they are doing, and 'pay for performance' rewards them for doing it.

London Life

Dr John Evans, sales manager of London Life Assurance described at the MCE conference in 1987 a turnover case which, inspired by a dynamic new chief executive, enabled a somewhat old-fashioned and sheltered company to achieve a 40 per cent growth rate per annum. When Dr Evans was appointed sales manager he found a sales force with high ethical values, who were stable, long-serving and productive, but who were not paid commission, were not led by skilled sales management and existed in a low profit sales and marketing environment. This environment or culture had to be changed and the methods used were to:

- Re-design the remuneration package to make it dependent on results.
- Set up a new career structure which meant that a highly successful salesman could earn more than his manager – in order to progress, the excellent salesman did not have to become a manager.
- Restructure management control in branches.
- Introduce crash management development and training.
- Introduce a new selection procedure designed to identify potential high-producing sales people, with the emphasis on commitment, initiative and reliability.

ACHIEVING EXCELLENCE

A number or recipes for achieving excellence have been developed recently and the following is a summary of the messages derived from three key studies.

In Search of Excellence

In Search of Excellence by Tom Peters and Robert Waterman (Harper & Row, 1982) is described in its sub-title as 'lessons from America's best-run companies'. The analytical framework they used was based on the seven elements, described as the 'seven Ss', which Richard Pascale and Anthony Athos used in *The Art of Japanese Management* (Simon and Schuster, 1981). These are:

1. *Strategy*: the plan to reach identified goals.
2. *Structure*: the characteristics of the organization structure – functional, decentralized etc.

3. *Systems*: the routine for processing and communicating information.
4. *Staff*: the categories of people employed.
5. *Style*: how managers behave in achieving the organization's goals.
6. *Skills*: the capabilities of key people.
7. *Superordinate goals*: the significant meanings or guiding concepts that an organization imbues in its members (ie values).

A distinction was made between the 'hard' elements – strategy, structure and systems – on which UK and American companies concentrate, and the remaining 'soft' elements which Pascale and Athos claimed the Japanese manage particularly well.

Using these factors in their research into 75 highly regarded companies Peters and Waterman identified the following eight attributes which characterized the excellent innovative companies:

1. *A bias for action*: the excellent companies get on with it. They are analytical in their decision making but this does not paralyse them, as it does in some companies.
2. *Close to the customer*: they get to know their customers and provide them with quality, reliability and service.
3. *Autonomy and entrepreneurship*: leaders and innovators are fostered and given scope.
4. *Productivity through people*: they really believe that the basis for quality and productivity gain is the rank and file. They do not just pay lip service to the slogan 'people are our most important asset'. They do something about it by encouraging commitment and getting everyone involved.
5. *Hands-on, value driven*: the people who run the organization get close to those who work for them and ensure that the organization's values are understood and acted upon.
6. *Stick to the knitting*: the successful organizations stay reasonably close to the businesses they know.
7. *Simple form, lean staff*: the organization structure is simple and corporate staff are kept to a minimum.
8. *Simultaneous loose-tight properties*: they are both decentralized and centralized. They push decisions and autonomy as far down the organization as they can get, into individual units and profit centres. But, as Peters and Waterman say, 'they are fanatic centralists around the few core values they hold dear'.

The Winning Streak

The Winning Streak by Walter Goldsmith and David Clutterbuck

(Weidenfeld and Nicholson, 1984) was based on an analysis of a number of successful British companies. From this they listed eight winning characteristics:

1. *Leadership*: this was regarded as central to business growth. As Goldsmith and Clutterbuck wrote: 'The business leader need not be charismatic (indeed, if he fails to combine charisma with wisdom, disaster is almost inevitable). But he must be able to motivate those around him, to provide a sense of mission for the organization as a whole, and to ensure that all the middle and junior management leaders down the line have clear objectives they can work to, to motivate and direct their own subordinates' efforts.'

2. *Autonomy*: this is giving people the freedom they need to do their job most effectively. The right blend has to be achieved between autonomy and control, and this varies a lot, even within one company.

3. *Control*: effective controls allow autonomy to take place. Neither too much nor too little is the aim; a balance must be struck. But rather a limited number of good controls than too many loose ones. As Tim Peters wrote: 'A few (controls) that are believed in are much more effective than numerous controls that are honoured mainly in the breach.'

4. *Involvement*: the successful companies extract a great deal of commitment and loyalty from staff at all levels. They do this by getting them closely involved with the organization and its aims.

5. *Market orientation*: as Goldsmith and Clutterbuck wrote: 'The unsuccessful companies lived in their markets; the successful ones lived them.'

6. *Getting back to basics and staying there*: winners know what business they are in and why they are in it; they know how to position it and target its market sector.

7. *Innovation*: successful companies create a climate which encourages innovation; they act on promising ideas.

8. *Integrity*: the best companies build up and maintain a reputation for fair dealing and trustworthiness with staff, customers, suppliers and the public at large.

The Business of Success

In *The Business of Success* (Sidgwick and Jackson, 1982) Robert Heller commented on the results of a study of 250 firms in the printing industry. The stars in this group, as measured by return on capital employed, ratio of profit to sales and value added, had five common features which make up the acronym OMMIT.

1. *Objectives*: business objectives were defined and the business operated to meet them.
2. *Market*: market opportunities were identified and commercial efforts co-ordinated to achieve planned business results.
3. *Money*: its role and use as a resource was clearly understood.
4. *Information*: there were good information systems in support of good decision-making procedures.
5. *Team*: management was organized to operate as a team, executives being developed to meet the changing needs of the business.

Heller said that any company omits any one of these factors at its peril. Note, however, that he did not specifically refer to people, but the effective management of human resources is implied in each one of them. Even money only gets results if *people* use it properly.

COMPANY CASE STUDIES

Hewlett-Packard

Hewlett- Packard is a highly successful multinational company with over 50,000 employees which develops and manufactures test instruments, computers, calculators, medical equipment and solid state components. It was one of the first of the large organizations that recognized the role HRM plays in shaping and reinforcing a company's culture.

The HRM programme started from a definition of Hewlett-Packard's objectives and the strategies for carrying them out. These were:

Objective	*Strategies for carrying out objectives*
Profit	Use reinvested profit to finance growth; strive to equate return on net worth with sales growth rate; avoid long-term loans.
Customers	Develop products based on customer needs and concerns; provide quality service on products; elicit customer input.
Fields of interest	Grow through related diversification; be innovative; temper innovativeness by considering ability to manufacture and market the products.

Growth	Limit growth only according to profit and ability to develop new products; hire high calibre people; compete for lead in field.
Our people	Provide employees opportunities to share in profits; avoid large production schedule fluctuation; employee recognition.
Management	Management by objectives; allow independent work; decentralized organization.
Citizenship	Concern for society's problems; employ and develop disadvantaged groups.

A number of cultural 'themes' were then developed and related to the objectives. The themes were:

1. *Familial atmosphere*: all employees should feel they belong to a corporate family. Decentralization and individual freedom are recognized as desirable, but a strong 'culture' is believed to be the key to tying all this diversification back together.
2. *The individual employee*: it is recognized that the individual is the source of the enthusiasm, initiative and labour that make the company what it is. Individuals are shown that they are to be trusted and are allowed a reasonable degree of independence.
3. *Inter-organizational co-operation*: co-operation between units and functions in a highly diversified operation is crucial to present customers with a 'one company' image and to allow successful internal integration.
4. *Entrepreneurial spirit*: creativity is an essential feature of the company and is encouraged in all employees.
5. *Management style*: management must engender trust in the employee, must stress the importance of the customer and must promote enthusiasm. This requires the dissolution of barriers between management and the rest of the organization.
6. *Hewlett-Packard pride*: employees must feel they play an important role in something important. The customer has to have faith in a company driven by pride. Workmanship must be of a standard of which everyone can be proud.
7. *Social neighbour*: the company has a commitment to the community and society.

8. *Profit*: a concern for profit plays an important role in the company's culture because much of its strategy hinges on making profit.

The system used to promote these themes or values includes:

- An open-door management policy and 'MBWA' – management by walking around.
- An emphasis on training and development.
- A results-oriented system of setting objectives and appraising performance against those objectives.
- A generous but egalitarian reward system with minimal management perks.

IBM

IBM operates successfully against the background of a well-formulated and understood set of basic beliefs. These are:

1. *Respect for the individual*: the dignity and the rights of each person in the organization.
2. *Customer service*: to give the best customer service of any company in the world.
3. *Excellence*: the conviction that an organization should pursue all tasks with the objective of accomplishing them in a superior way.

In addition to these basic beliefs there are a set of fundamental principles which guide IBM management in the conduct of the business. They are:

- To give intelligent, responsible, and capable direction to the business.
- To serve our customers as efficiently and as effectively as we can.
- To advance our technology, improve our products and develop new ones.
- To enlarge the capabilities of our people through job development and give them the opportunity to find satisfaction in their tasks.
- To provide equal opportunity to all our people.
- To recognize our obligation to stockholders by providing adequate return on their investment.
- To do our part in furthering the well-being of those communities in which our facilities are located.
- To accept our responsibilities as a corporate citizen of the US and in all the countries throughout the world in which we operate.

Honeywell – Aerospace and Defence Business (ADB)

In 1987 the ADB division of Honeywell had defined its philosophy of management in the statement 'Our Way' as follows:

> We believe that successful accomplishment of ADB's business goals and of our own personal goals requires a high level of awareness, involvement, and co-operation by all.
>
> Our way of achieving this is through the advancement of mutual trust, high self-esteem, and team goal-setting, along with high standards of performance and a firm commitment to the highest quality of work.
>
> A work environment which fosters openness, fulfilment, and the mutual utilization of everyone's unique talents and responsibilities is essential to reach our goals.
>
> In this way, we will be able to meet our customers' needs and bring meaningful rewards to ourselves, our company, and our community.

To get this philosophy working effectively it was decided that an action research programme was required to integrate the large number of human resource activities already in place into the organization's strategic business plan. The programme was conducted in association with the University of Michigan's action research team headed by Noel Tichy.

The research highlighted three main strategic areas for development:

1. *Technical*: top level managers needed agreement on the strategic development of ADB.
2. *Political*: succession issues were becoming increasingly important. ADB needed a better process for effectively managing succession politics.
3. *Cultural*: the organization was not perceived as having a culture consistent with the 'Our Way' statement, hence a 'culture strategy was needed'. In addition, various aspects of the human resource management cycle (selection, appraisal, rewards, and training and development) were seen as points of concern.

The main action programmes instituted to implement a strategic approach to human resource management were:

1. *Strategic planning changes*: the business strategic planning process in ADB needed to be improved. Human resource considerations should be incorporated in the formulation of strategy and human resource activities should be viewed as a means of business strategy implementation.
2. *Human resource planning changes*: the key to change in this area

was to build on the strength that already existed. The existing talent review process, which covered only the top 10 per cent, should be extended to include all key positions. The review should require managers to address the following issues several times a year:
- the organization of their business to support the strategic plan;
- their human resource needs.
3. *Development of employee relations staff*: the employee relations department staff should be much more involved in the strategic planning process.

Volvo – Holland

The 'new style' programme of management was introduced by Volvo in Holland in 1974. Ten years later production had doubled and, more importantly, so had sales, while the size of the labour force remained virtually unchanged.

At the heart of this programme was the definition by Volvo of the business they were in: not just producing cars; instead, they produced a model with variants, which was targeted very specifically at the executive or professional customer who wanted some luxury, a fairly 'sporty' image and high quality. This provided the theme for a campaign, starting at the top, which aimed at indoctrinating all employees – managers and workers alike – in the need to achieve high standards of quality as well as output. The process was one of continuous education coupled with clear definitions of what was expected of everyone, and the provision of ample opportunities to contribute to the improvement of performance.

HOW THEY DID IT

The following four cases illustrate how individuals can create the conditions in an organization which enable it to achieve success.

Harold S Geenen

Harold S Geenen was the highly successful chief executive of the International Telephone and Telegraph Company (ITT) for 17 years. His business philosophy was summed up in his book *Managing* by his three-sentence course on business management: 'You read a book from beginning to end. You run a business in the opposite way. You start with the end, and then you do everything you must to reach it.' His emphasis was on setting goals, quarter by quarter (his most famous memo at ITT was: 'There will be no more long-range planning'), and then monitoring performance closely through an open system of communications. Reports on key business operations went straight to him and he personally reviewed with divisional chief executives their results on the spot.

When he first took on the job of chief executive he set out to restructure the company from a loosely held, sluggish holding company into an integrated, well-managed entity. To do this he got hold of the best people he could, paid them over the odds and expected them to perform. He stressed the need to cut through the formal structure so the managers of the autonomous subsidiaries would think of ITT as 'one company, one team, one group of management men heading in the same direction'.

Effective leadership and support from the top was seen by Geenen to be all important. When his monitoring system was first introduced, it caused fear and resentment among his divisional executives. But they recognized and accepted the fact that it was there so that headquarters could help them succeed in their line operations; and that when they succeeded, with or without the help of headquarters, they would receive full credit for their achievement. He summed it all up by saying: 'The climate control is in the hands of the chief executive.'

Lee Iacocca

Lee Iacocca was invited to become Chrysler's chief executive in 1978. The company was in a crisis, but he turned it round. How did he do it? In his own words: 'In the end, all business operations can be reduced to three words: people, product, and profits. People come first. Unless you've got a good team, you can't do much with the other two.' Fine words, but many successful chief executives have said much the same thing. How was Iacocca different?

Clearly, he is a man who knows his own mind and has the strength of purpose to get what he wants. But he did achieve this through people. His first act was to build a new team. He did this either by recruiting people he knew could do the job he wanted or by building up the strengths of any able people who were already employed by Chrysler. He then weeded out the people who would not fit in the new organization; tough, but in the circumstances, necessary. With the right people around, his next step was to ensure that they knew what had to be done, by themselves personally, and by their staff. He therefore introduced the quarterly review system which had worked well for him at the Ford Motor Company. He asked his key people, and ensured that they asked *their* key people, and so on down the line, three basic questions:

1. What are your objectives for the next 90 days?

2. What are your plans, priorities and hopes?
3. How do you intend to go about achieving them?

He got all his managers to sit down every three months to discuss these questions and agree on answers to them. The outcome of these meetings was put down in writing, on the grounds that the discipline of writing something down is the first step toward making it happen.

Superimposed on this process of objective setting and review was Iacocca's vision, which he conveyed to the people who worked for him. He was quite clear that 'management is nothing more than motivating other people' and that is what he succeeded in doing. Of course, he had to pick the right people – 'the eager beavers' – and he had to give them scope. As he said about his dozen top managers:

> What makes these managers strong is that they know how to delegate and how to motivate. They know how to look for the pressure points and how to set priorities. They're the kind of guys who can say 'Forget that, it'll take ten years. Here's what we gotta do now.'

Ed Carlson

Ed Carlson successfully turned United Airlines around using the following principles of HRM:

1. *People orientation*: Carlson's system reflected that the head of any organization, while influencing his subordinates, had to treat them as respected and trusted. He shared Chester Barnard's view that employees in a sense delegate upwards to management the authority for organizational decisions, and in so doing legitimize the right of those above to command those below.
2. *Visible management*: the cornerstone of Carlson's system was that employees of the company ought to see the man who is in charge. He embarked on a communication programme which was to become his trademark. He encouraged employees to talk to him personally and gave straight answers to tough questions. His objective was to sell his goals to the employees themselves. He did his best to minimize the problem of what he called NETMA – nobody tells me anything.
3. *Decentralization*: Carlson decentralized operations into three competing divisions, but he invited managers to a retreat to go through plans thoroughly and thus ensure full commitment.
4. *Base touching*: the approach was to work through people, not by giving orders, but by selling people on the merits of the programme and its logic and goals. Carlson made a habit of sounding people

out on new ideas by consulting subordinates in informal face-to-face meetings.

5. *A drive for information*: Carlson had a craving for information, and in United Airlines the key to implementable decisions was not only to track down the facts, but also to get the key people to agree what those facts meant and what should be done about them.

6. *Participative planning and control*: an elaborate planning and control system was instituted. But it was used as a context for dialogue, not just as a mechanism.

7. *Support for senior executives:* Carlson trusted his top executives. He deliberately sought a diversity of styles and ideas in the managers around him. It was said of him by one of his senior managers: 'His mixture of pressure and praise commanded loyalty. He was informal without being chummy, hard driving but easy mannered, interested in his aides as people without being patronizing. He treated us more like colleagues or associates than employees.'

8. *Team huddles*: a final characteristic of Carlson's system of management was its emphasis on consensus. Most top level decisions were made in the open at meetings.

John Harvey-Jones

In 1982 John Harvey-Jones became chairman of ICI – a massive but then an ailing business, profits before tax in 1981 being £325 million. In his words, it was 'growing barnacles'. When he retired in 1987 he left behind a thriving business making £1 billion profit, together with an organization that was less hierarchical, less bureaucratic and able to respond quickly to change.

How did he achieve this turn-round? His methods can be summarized as follows:

1. *Overall philosophy*: 1) the organization had to be capable of renewing itself constantly; 2) small units are more manageable than big ones; 3) the individual matters.

2. *Managing change*: change percolated through ICI by a cascade effect. The board set the pace and everyone else took up the baton. The aim was to get every individual to see his own place in relation to the rest of the company and from this picture glean an idea of his part in the changes that were taking place. This would take the fear out of change – and that is the biggest brake on individuals embracing new ideas. Harvey-Jones made the point that: 'people have first to decide that they want to change, then they must be

encouraged not to be afraid of change, and finally they must be able to see where change is leading them'.

3. *Organization*: the organization had to be continually adaptive. All large organizations have tendencies towards creeping centralization and top-heavy bureaucracy, and this inhibits innovation and change. Harvey-Jones approached this problem by relaxing the grip of the centre and thus giving people 'headroom to grow'. He put the decision-making authority back into the hands of the people who were competent to exercise it. As he said: 'How the hell can I know whether the guy in India should be changing his product, or whether somebody in Australia should be changing his technology? People don't like centralization because it uses them like machines.'

4. *Control*: decentralization did not, however, mean lack of control. 'While we've set businesses free to pursue their own objectives, the controls have actually got more rigid. We only manage on a small number of parameters, but they are pretty ruthless.'

5. *Leadership*: Harvey-Jones believed that managers must be persuaders and communicators; they have to ensure that their staff understand issues and have the information to make their own judgements. 'There's nothing easier than to stand on the bridge shouting instructions. But absolutely nothing happens unless people believe that what you're doing is right. What I want is a federation of freemen working together of their own free will for a socially decent common cause.'

6. *Management style*: openness and bluntness began to shake up the long-established but over-managed company and out went 'ritual dancing, weasel words and politicking'. Polite conformity was discouraged and 'tolerance of difference' preferred.

3. Organization Design

WHAT IS ORGANIZATION DESIGN?

Human resources are organized to do what the enterprise wants them to do. Organization design could be described as deciding who does what in order to get the right things done. But there is more to it than that: relationships and interrelationships have to be clarified – who does what with whom; authorities must be defined – who says what has to be done. The organization design will be affected by four factors:

1. The situation in which the organization exists – internal and environmental factors.
2. Organizational dynamics – the impact of change.
3. The impact of information technology.
4. Organizational choice arising from the situation dynamics, technology and complexity.

Situational factors

Organizations exist to get things done. The organization itself is an entity which is there for a purpose, which determines what it sets out to do. But *what* it actually does and *how* it actually does it will be influenced by a number of external and internal forces. These include the environment and the sort of organization it is – its reason for existence and history, its culture, values, management style, customers or clients.

Organizational dynamics

Forming and developing an organization which will make the best use of the human resources available to it is a complex and dynamic process. As Alfred P Sloan put it in *My Years With General Motors*: 'Change is the only thing that remains constant in organizations.' Change is imposed by the business, economic, political, legal and social environment. It is also generated within the enterprise: by innovation and development on the part of management or by movements of people into or out of the organization.

The impact of information technology

It can be argued that communication is the basis of organization. The word communication derives from the Latin word *communis,* which means sharing; people in organizations can only work co-operatively together if they share information.

Information technology, especially where it involves networking with the extensive use of personal computers working from a common database, can have a significant effect on organizational effectiveness – for good or for ill. For good if it is planned with the needs of the organization and the people in it fully in mind. For ill if it is imposed on the system by data processing experts who do not appreciate the impact of their systems on the organization.

Paul Strassman, formerly with Xerox, goes so far as to say that the organization of the future is a structure in which information flow serves as the central design principle. He makes the point that you should never allow computer people to design information systems that shape organization structures by default. You should always use information technology to make possible organizational forms that simplify delivery of the products and services to customers. Proposals for extending networks should be scrutinized to ensure that with their help, people will be able to co-operate and share knowledge better.

Organizational complexity and choice

Organizations can be complex operations because the people who work in them and the environment with which they interact are complex. There are seldom simple solutions to organizational problems, and what appears to be simple can, in practice, prove to be simplistic. There is almost always a choice in how to organize, and the obvious answer may not be the best one. To organize is to compromise. There may be an ideal solution to an organizational problem but you will seldom achieve it. People get in the way. You may plan to get where you want to be but you are unlikely ever to get there. Changes take place. You cannot impose principles on how to organize: there are no such things as principles of organization; there are only guidelines, based on empirical evidence of what has worked elsewhere, but even these have to be adapted to the peculiar circumstances existing in your organization.

THE PROCESS OF ORGANIZATION DESIGN

The process of organization design can be defined as the design, development and maintenance of a system of co-ordinated activities in which individuals and groups work co-operatively under authority and leadership towards commonly understood and accepted goals. However, this definition does not really tell you what you have to do. You have to do far more than just drawing up organization charts and writing job descriptions. There are five basic organization questions that need to be answered:

1. What business are we in?
2. What are we setting out to do?
3. What work needs to be done and by whom, ie who does what?
4. How should individual jobs be designed and enriched?
5. How should the business be structured?

Note the sequence of questions. Deciding who does what and defining the structure follow the fundamental requirements to define the business and determine its objectives. The structure should emerge from these considerations, and then more work has to be done, along the lines described in Chapter 1 and later chapters, to ensure that it functions effectively and flexibly in response to external and internal pressures and change.

WHAT BUSINESS ARE WE IN?

This is the famous question posed by Peter Drucker as long ago as 1955 in his classic *The Practice of Management*. The important thing to do is to define the business in terms of the customer or client. As Drucker wrote: 'What is our business is not defined by the producer, but by the consumer.' He went on to say that: 'It is then the first responsibility of top management to ask the question "What is our business?" and to make sure that it is carefully studied and correctly answered.'

The president of American Telephone and Telegraph stated that, 'Our business is service' and Charles Revson, the founder of Revlon, said, 'In the factory we make cosmetics. In the store we sell hope.' Publishers who just think they are in the business of producing and selling books will lose out. They have to see themselves as being in the leisure and/or the information business. Robert Heller, in *The Business of Success*, found that in a study of 350 firms in the printing business, 80 per cent of the successful firms specialized in one or more market areas. They did not just say, 'We're in printing', instead they stated, for example, that, 'We supply labels to wine companies'.

Peters and Waterman in *In Search of Excellence* said that the excellent organizations 'stick to the knitting'. In other words they build their business round a single skill; the coating and bonding technology at 3M, for example. And that skill is related directly to the market. Management keeps its 'feel' and becomes entirely credible down the line because managers can say 'I was there'. Herzberg says that motivation is strongest in companies where managers and workers are in close and constant touch with their customer or client, which is only possible if they know who their real customer is and what he or she needs. In other words, they know the business they are in.

WHAT ARE WE SETTING OUT TO DO?

This question is answered by strategic planning, as mentioned in Chapter 1. The aims of strategic planning are to:

- Define and plan the long-term future of the company as a whole.
- Increase the rate of growth of the enterprise in the long run.
- Ensure that the organization can meet the challenge of change and can profit from new opportunities.

The process of strategic planning

Strategic planning is carried out in the following stages:

1. Set objectives which define what the company is and what it is setting out to do, in terms of growth in sales and revenue and profit, and in return on capital employed.
2. Prepare long-range forecasts based upon present strategies. These will identify any gaps between the objectives and targets as set at stage 1 and indicate the extent to which new or revised strategies are required.
3. Define broad strategies to achieve objectives, bearing in mind any gaps revealed by the analysis at stage 2.
4. Create financial, marketing, capital investment, acquisition, diversification and human resource and product development plans to implement strategies.
5. Monitor results against the plans and amend strategies or take corrective action as necessary.

WHO DOES WHAT?

This is the fundamental organization question you have to answer when you complete your basic analysis. You start by looking at what needs to be done and then decide who does it. But the what and the who are inextricably linked. In theory, you analyse what has to be done and then fit in the people. In practice, the people you have got, in the short term, or the people you can get, in the longer term, will exert influence on what can be done. The amount of influence exerted will be governed by the extent to which the work done is affected by individual skills and expertise rather than by established routines.

What needs to be done?

The sort of business you are in, the objectives set for that business, and the approach you adopt to achieving excellence will determine the work that needs to be done. A systematic and continuous analysis of the activities required is essential.

Three basic questions need answering:

1. What are the main activities carried out in the enterprise?
2. Are all the activities required to achieve objectives properly catered for?
3. Are any unnecessary activities being carried out?

When you analyse the existing range of activities you should classify them by:

- The product or service with which the activity is concerned.
- The users of that product or service.
- The type of activity, for example, marketing, selling, manufacturing, quality control, distribution, administration, or providing advice and assistance.
- The degree to which the work is continuous, subject to change, routine or innovative.
- The type of production system in use – unit, mass, process, batch or flow.
- The extent to which the work demands professional or technical expertise.

When considering the activities that should be carried out you should check particularly on those concerned with:

- Formulating, agreeing and reviewing objectives, policies and plans.
- Conducting product, technical, market, economic or social research.
- Developing products, markets or services.
- Preparing financial forecasts and evaluations.
- Providing management information and systems for monitoring performance.

- Providing specialist, professional or technical advice and services in such areas as personnel management, quality control, data processing, process development, productivity planning and financial planning.
- Integrating related activities.
- Co-ordinating and controlling complex operations.
- Communicating information to employees, shareholders and the public.

Who does it?

The activity analysis tells you what is and is not being done, and what ought to be done. You then need to conduct a human resource analysis to provide answers to the following questions:

1. For individual managers, professional staff and technologists: who is doing what at present? how well are they doing it? to what extent have responsibilities been adjusted to fit individual capacities, strengths or weaknesses, and how far have any such adjustments been justified?
2. For key categories of staff, eg managers, professional, technologists, supervisors, sales, manufacturing, data processing, finance, research and development: are they adequate with regard to numbers and quality to meet present demands, and any future demands arising from re-organization?

The answers to these questions will provide you with guidance on the extent to which an ideal allocation of responsibilities may have to be modified because of the special nature of the qualities of people either currently in jobs or available to take on other duties.

The analysis of who does what, however, is only the first stage in organization planning. It provides the basic information, but you have to go on from there to consider how best to design and enrich individual jobs. To get the work done effectively *and* to motivate the job holders, these jobs have then to be fitted into an organization structure.

JOB DESIGN AND ENRICHMENT

Job design

Job design is the process of deciding on the content of a job in terms of its duties and responsibilities; on the methods to be used in carrying out the job, in terms of techniques, systems and procedures; and on the relationships that should exist between the job holder and his/her superiors, subordinates and colleagues.

The aims of job design are:

1. To satisfy the requirements of the organization for productivity, operational efficiency and quality of product or services.
2. To satisfy the needs of the individual for interest, challenge and accomplishment.

Clearly, these aims are interrelated and the overall objective of job design is to integrate the needs of the individual with those of the organization.

The process of job design starts from an analysis of what work needs to be done – tasks that have to be carried out if the purpose of the organization or an organizational unit is to be achieved. This is where the techniques of work study, process planning and organizational analysis are used. Inevitably, these techniques are directed to the first aim of job design: the maximization of efficiency and productivity. They concentrate on the work to be done, not the worker. They may lead to a high degree of task specialization and assembly line processing, of paper work as well as physical products. This, in turn, can lead to the minimization of individual responsibility and the opportunity to use personal skills.

Job design starts from an analysis of work requirements, but when the tasks to be done have been determined it is the function of the job designer to consider how the jobs can be set up to provide the maximum degree of intrinsic motivation for those who have to carry them out. Consideration has also to be given to another implied aim of job design, which is to fulfil the social responsibilities of the organization to the people who work in it by improving the quality of working life, which depends upon both efficiency of performance and satisfaction of the worker. For this purpose, you should consider using job enrichment techniques.

Job enrichment

Job enrichment maximizes the interest and challenge of work by providing the employee with a job that has these characteristics:

- It is a complete piece of work in the sense that the worker can identify a series of tasks or activities that end in a recognizable and definable product.
- It affords the employee as much variety, decision-making responsibility and control as possible in carrying out the work.
- It provides direct feedback through the work itself on how well the employee is doing his/her job.

Job enrichment is not just increasing the number or variety of tasks, neither is it the provision of opportunities for job rotation. These approaches may relieve boredom, but they do not result in positive increases in motivation.

There is no one way of enriching a job. The technology and the circumstances will dictate which of the following techniques or combination of techniques is appropriate:

- Increasing the responsibility of individuals for their own work.
- Giving employees more scope to vary the methods, sequence and pace of their work.
- Giving a person or a work group a complete natural unit of work, ie reducing task specialization.
- Removing some controls from above while ensuring that individuals or groups are clearly accountable for achieving defined targets or standards.
- Allowing employees more influence in setting targets and standards of performance.
- Giving employees the control information they need to monitor their own performance.
- Encouraging the participation of employees in planning work, innovating new techniques and reviewing results.
- Introducing new and more difficult tasks not previously handled.
- Assigning individuals or groups specific projects which give them more responsibility and help them to increase their expertise.

You should take the following steps when introducing job enrichment:

1. Select those jobs where better motivation is most likely to improve performance.
2. Set up a controlled pilot scheme before launching the full programme of job enrichment.
3. Brainstorm a list of changes that may enrich the jobs, without concern at this stage for their practicability.
4. Screen the list to concentrate on motivation factors such as achievement, responsibility and self-control.
5. Ensure that the changes are not just generalities like 'increase responsibility', but list specific differences in the way in which the jobs are designed and carried out.
6. Set precise objectives and criteria for measuring success and a timetable for each project, and ensure that control information is available to monitor progress and the results achieved.

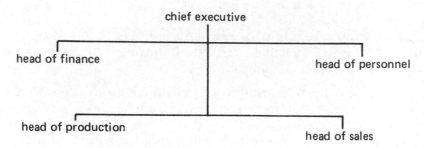

Figure 3.1 *Conventional structure*

STRUCTURING THE ORGANIZATION

The structure of an organization is the framework for getting things done. The process of structuring or re-structuring is essentially about grouping activities and establishing authorities and relationships.

The conventional structure is sometimes called a line and staff organization. There is a direct line of command for those in the 'line' functions, which are primarily concerned with achieving the objectives of the organization, eg production and sales. Staff positions are also created which exist to give advice and services to the line, eg finance and personnel. The structure will be drawn up as shown in Figure 3.1.

An alternative form of organization is the matrix organization, which exists when the operation is based on projects, as in a research and development department or a management consultancy. Project managers lead interdisciplinary teams, the members of which are assigned to them for the duration of the project, but these individuals are responsible on a continuing basis to the heads of their own discipline. A matrix structure will be drawn up as shown in Figure 3.2.

project team \ discipline	a	b	c	d
A	x	x		x
B		x	x	x
C	x		x	x
D	x	x	x	

Figure 3.2 *Matrix structure*

Aims

If you are looking at an existing structure or thinking about a new structure, you should have the following aims:

Activities

The aim should be to group activities logically together. Like should be linked with like and there should be a common purpose. But these two subsidiary aims are not always compatible. It might seem logical to group similar manufacturing processes together to achieve economies of scale and concentration of skills or facilities. However, this could militant against the equally, possibly, more desirable objective of linking the activities needed to make and sell a product in a specified market to form a profit centre for which clear accountability could be allocated.

Activities should be grouped together in a way which facilitates control and ensures that individuals can be held accountable for achieving defined objectives. Grouping should also take account of the need to co-ordinate activities. It should attempt to minimize the boundary problems that inevitably arise among activities which, although interdependent, may have different ideas of priorities, standards and timetables and between which there may be rivalry; for example, manufacturing and sales.

Accountability

The concept of accountable management is, or should be, a fundamental part of any approach to organization. It means people knowing what they have to achieve and being held responsible for the results they obtain. Accountable management is discussed in more detail later in this chapter.

From a structural point of view, accountability is enhanced if everyone knows exactly to whom he is responsible and for what, and has an equally clear understanding of who is responsible, in turn, to him and for what. The belief that one man cannot have two bosses is valid in so far as it can create confusion as to where priorities and responsibilities lie. This is not, however, an absolutely rigid principle. Individuals should indeed only have 'line' responsibility, ie direct responsibility for achieving the key objectives of the job, to one boss. But they could also be subjected to a degree of 'staff' authority from those in specialist areas such as finance, quality control, or personnel management.

Managers or officials in those or similar areas may necessarily be charged with the responsibility of ensuring that corporate procedures, policies or standards are adhered to. A machinist, for example, is responsible to his line foreman for achieving both output and quality standards, but a staff inspector can reject work which is not up to standard. Conflict between line and staff can be minimized, although not always avoided, by carefully defining authorities and providing for appeals to be lodged against apparently unreasonable staff decisions at a higher level.

A 'matrix' system of organization, as discussed earlier, may make individuals responsible to both their project manager and the head of their own discipline. Confusion can be minimized in these circumstances by making it clear that so far as the project is concerned, the individual it totally responsible to the project manager. The head of his own discipline can provide guidance on standards but cannot give instructions on how the particular project should be carried out. On a continuing basis and between projects, however, the head of the function is responsible for the individual's overall performance, training, development, discipline and remuneration, and also for assigning him to projects.

Control

The structure must facilitate control, which means seeing that what should be done is done. Control involves measuring results against plans, targets or budgets and then taking any corrective action required. It need not be rigid in the sense of looking at every detail, but it must concentrate on the key performance areas.

Good control depends primarily on individuals being given clearly defined accountability and the authority to ensure that they get the information they need to take action. Structurally, control is easier if the number of subordinates reporting directly to one individual – the 'span of control' – is limited to the number he can control satisfactorily.

There is no magic number for the optimum span of control. It depends on the range of activities managed and the extent to which there are significant differences between the responsibilities of the various subordinates. A chief executive may not be able to exercise proper control over more than six or seven subordinates, if each is responsible for a separate area of activity; but a foreman supervising workers on a routine assembly line could control 20 staff quite satisfactorily.

A span of control can be too small. If a manager has only two subordinates, he is likely to interfere too much with what they do. He might even polarize his attention on one area of activity at the expense of another. An example of this was an organization which was rapidly running into a state of insolvency. There were only two executives reporting to the chief executive and he, a marketing man, concentrated far more on the work of the director of operations than that of the director of finance. The latter area was neglected, the company over-traded, and serious cash flow problems occurred.

Effective control can also be endangered if you have too many levels of management and supervision between the chief executive and the main working force. It is possible for companies to be over-managed. Unnecessary layers of management hinder communications and result in overlapping and confused areas of authority.

A regionalized sales organization was structured with four levels of management and supervision between the marketing director and sales representatives in the field. The responsibilities of each layer – sales manager, regional sales manager, area manager, district manager – were not clear. The sales representatives did not know what they were expected to achieve in terms of sales turnover and contribution targets for each of their product lines. The marketing director had no idea what was really happening in the field, except that he was not getting the results he needed.

The system and structure for control must not inhibit decision making. Top management should know what is happening in the key result areas so that they can monitor performance and guide the enterprise in the right direction. But they must also decentralize and delegate decision making as close to the point of action as they can, consistent with exercising a reasonable degree of overall control.

Co-ordination
The structure should provide for effective co-ordination by grouping activities appropriately together and by limiting spans of control to manageable proportions. Other methods of achieving integration are discussed later in this chapter.

Communications
You should take into account the need to maintain good communications across departmental boundaries, eg between production and sales, when grouping activities. Over-rigid boundaries create communication problems and, as noted above, so do too many levels of management.

You should always remember that, while the organization chart may purport to define lines of communication, there will and must be informal channels. Any attempt to restrict contacts to the formal network will induce rigor mortis in the organization.

A balance needs to be struck between over-formality and the chaos that can result if normal channels are continuously ignored. The extent to which informality can be allowed depends largely upon the kind of organization. In a bureaucratic type of concern, such as a government department or an insurance company, formality may have to prevail in order to regularize decision making in accordance with set procedures. A more fluid type of organization, such as a research and development establishment, will benefit from a reasonable degree of tolerance towards informality.

Flexibility

We live in turbulent times. Most organizations exist in a state of continuous change; they have to respond to new demands, and this means coping with sudden alterations to responsibilities and structures. You have to be prepared to reorganize frequently in any environment where change is a constant factor.

The old jibe, 'organize - reorganize - disorganize', may have some validity if change is made for change's sake - and this happens. Consultants are brought in and produce the parrot cry 'decentralization'. Extra and unnecessary layers of management are created, as in the disastrous reorganization of the British health service a few years ago. The result is a modified form of chaos, and back we go to centralization.

This pendulum process in organizations is a well-known pheno-menon: 'Those behind cried "forward!" and those before cried "back!".' It can be avoided without resorting to rigidity if organizational changes, although made rapidly in response to events, are based on a proper analysis of the situation and are not governed by some fad of a chief executive or a management consultant.

Methods: overall approach

Essentially, when you organize or reorganize something, you are going through a process of differentiation followed by one of integration. You start by differentiating each of the key activities required to achieve the objectives of the enterprise. You then proceed to integrate them so that all the different parts work smoothly together to fulfil the aims of the organization.

Organizing can be likened to selecting a set of bricks - the activities - and then putting them together to form a well-bonded structure which will be fit for its purpose. But there is not one right way of building the structure; there is always organizational choice. This choice arises because the aims and guidelines mentioned earlier often conflict with one another. For example, better control can be achieved by reducing the number of subordinates responsible directly to one manager, or by reducing the number of levels of supervision beneath him; but these alternatives are clearly inconsistent. If you have the same number of distinct activities, squeezing down the span of control will almost inevitably increase the number of layers, and reducing the number of layers will increase the span of control. A balance has to be struck and where this happens will be a matter of choice. You will make the best choice if you have thoroughly analysed the situation and evaluated each alternative course of action.

There is a further complication. The type of organization required will be dependent – contingent – upon the situation, and the situation will be a function of the type of business you are in and the technology and systems you use. For example, a large mail order company selling a range of related groups of products will have a 'business generation' division which buys, markets and promotes each range. Each major department – buying, marketing and catalogue – will contribute in various ways to the success of a product range. Close co-operation, coupled with a fluid approach to dealing with problems, will be essential. Business will be conducted aggressively, opportunism will prevail and quick reactions will be essential. The type of people who succeed in this environment will be those who can tolerate change, varying pressures and a measure of ambiguity.

Methods of doing work, the people who do the work and the form of organization will be quite different in the customer service departments which are processing orders and distributing goods to customers. Here, arrangements will be orderly, efficient and programmed to meet deadlines and follow precise routines. The system, the people and the structure will have to fit this environment.

Form follows function. In other words, what is done determines how it is done. If the function is not understood and the form or structure is not fitted appropriately to it, the organization will not work as effectively as it should.

The human factor will exert further influence on the organization. This consists of three elements:

1. *The people* themselves who work in the organization; the skills and capacities they possess and their attitude to the company.
2. *The management style* prevalent in the organization, which usually stems from the top. The style may be aggressive, authoritarian, democratic or *laissez-faire*. Whichever it is, it will affect the way people work as individuals or in groups.
3. *The organizational climate*, the atmosphere which exists in the company. People may be more or less co-operative. Conflict may be open but quickly resolved, or it may fester in corners. People may or may not trust one another. Political manoeuvrings may be rife, or everything may be done out in the open and in a straightforward way.

The human factor affects structure simply because some managers will be capable of undertaking a wide span of activities, while others may have to have the scope of their responsibilities limited. It could also affect the organization in more subtle ways. Individual behaviour, management style and the climate will influence the way the organization works. They will establish an informal organization which, for good or for ill, will operate in a different way from that planned into the formal structure. For good, possibly, because it will oil the wheels, help to cut corners and generally get things done. For ill, possibly, because it might interfere with and confuse the normal processes of control and co-ordination.

Method of proceeding

What emerges from this discussion of factors affecting organization is the need systematically to collect the facts about the organization before considering alternative structures. The steps you should take when organizing or reorganizing are therefore as follows:

1. Analyse the situation, covering these points:
   - the business the company is in;
   - the objectives of the business;
   - the activities that are needed to achieve objectives;
   - the environmental influences, eg the amount of competition, the extent to which trading is carried out in turbulent or unpredictable conditions;
   - the technologies or methods of operation used in the organization, with particular reference to the extent to which they are routine and predictable or varied and subject to change;
   - the people in the organization; to what extent has the organization been built around existing strengths or weaknesses, and to what extent and for how long will any future structure have to be adjusted to fit the availability of people and their capacities?
   - the management style;
   - the organizational culture, values and climate.
2. List and evaluate alternative structures – ways of grouping activities and allocating responsibilities to individual job holders.
3. Select the alternative which, on balance, is most likely to be effective. This may be a compromise in the short term. The ideal longer-term solution may only be achievable by degrees because of the need to move existing people or to find new people.
4. Prepare an implementation plan, which may have to be staged. The implementation will have to cover informing people of the new arrangements – and they will get a mixed reception, depending on how individuals are affected by them. Obviously, the aim will be to

explain why the changes are necessary and to minimize any unnecessary fears. The implementation plan will also have to deal with any training or re-training required and the actions necessary to engage new people or to redeploy existing staff.

5. Create and implement an organization development programme, as described in the next chapter, to ensure that you have a healthy and effective organization.

4. Organization Development

THE NEED AND AIMS

A human resources organization programme starts by paying attention to the corporate culture and its values – re-shaping or re-defining them as necessary. Against this background you can design an organization structure, but you have to make it function effectively, and this is what organization development is about.

The aim of an organization development (OD) programme is to improve the effectiveness with which an organization functions and responds to change.

The effective organization

As defined by Richard Beckhard, an effective organization is one in which:

1. The total organization, the significant subparts and individuals, manage their work against goals and plans, for achievement of these goals.
2. Form follows function (the problem, task, or project determines how the human resources are organized).
3. Decisions are made by and near the sources of information, regardless of where these sources are located on the organization chart.
4. The reward system is such that managers and supervisors are rewarded (and punished) comparably for: short-term profit or production performance; growth and development of their subordinates; and creating a viable working group.
5. Communication laterally and vertically is relatively undistorted. People are generally open and confrontational. They share all the relevant facts, including feelings.
6. There is a minimum amount of inappropriate win/lose activities

between individuals and groups. Constant effort exists at all levels to treat conflict and conflict situations as problems subject to problem-solving methods.

7. There is high 'conflict' (clash of ideas) about tasks and projects, and relatively little energy spent in clashing over interpersonal difficulties because they have generally been worked through.

8. The organization and its parts see themselves as interacting with each other and with a larger environment. The organization is an 'open system'.

9. There is a shared value, and management strategy to support it, of trying to help each person (or unit) in the organization maintain his (or its) integrity and uniqueness in an interdependent environment.

10. The organization and its members operate in an 'action-research' way. General practice is to build in feedback mechanisms so that individuals and groups can learn from their own experience.

ORGANIZATION DEVELOPMENT METHODS

Organization development programmes have the following main features:

- They are managed or at least strongly supported from the top, but may make use of third parties or 'change agents' to diagnose problems and achieve improvement or manage change by various kinds of planned activity or 'intervention'.
- The plans for organization development are based upon a systematic analysis and diagnosis of the circumstances of the organization and the changes and problems affecting it.
- They deal with how the organization copes in times of change with such processes as interaction, communication, participation planning and conflict.

ORGANIZATION DEVELOPMENT ACTIVITIES

The aspects of the way in which an organization functions which are particularly relevant in human resource organization programmes are:

- Co-ordination and integration.
- Teamwork.
- Managing conflict.
- Managing change.
- Achieving commitment.

Co-ordination and integration

The co-ordination and integration of activities in an organization does not just happen; it has to be worked at. People tend to head off in different directions – to go their own sweet way. They will not necessarily co-operate with one another. Good co-ordination is partly a structural matter. It is helpful if activities are grouped logically together, lines of communication are short and well-defined, and managers do not have unwieldy spans of control, but there are additional approaches you can adopt to achieve better integration. These include:

- *Voluntary integration*: encourage people to communicate with each other and to integrate their activities without reference to higher authority, except where a decision is needed to resolve differences of opinion.
- *Meetings*: set up meetings or committees to deal with planning and operational matters requiring integration. To avoid the dangers inherent in 'management by committee' you should ensure that meetings concentrate on resolving policy issues where joint decisions are required, rather than attempting to usurp the normal role of management.
- *Project teams*: set up teams or working parties to deal with specific issues or problems outside the normal routine; for example, product development, quality control and systems development. Getting people from different departments to work together is a good way of increasing understanding and developing a sense of common purpose.
- *Communications*: improve the quality of communications throughout the organization. This is partly a matter of attitude (there has to be the will to communicate and to listen to communications), partly a matter of structure (too many levels of management or too many separate units or departments will inhibit communications), and partly a matter of the systems and techniques used (the more effective use of the spoken or written word). All this is easier said than done. You cannot force people to communicate; you can only encourage them and try to remove barriers of misunderstanding.
- *Training*: train people to make them more aware of the need to integrate and to improve communication and leadership techniques. Courses attended by members of different departments can increase understanding. Team-building training, which concentrates on helping people to work better together in groups, is useful.
- *Understanding of roles*: help interrelated functions, units and individuals to be aware of their respective roles. This can be

achieved by various informal means, as mentioned above. You can also produce more formal definitions and circulate them to all concerned, but this seldom works: it is just possible that the missives will be read by the recipients, although it is most unlikely that they will take any notice of impersonal exhortations. Management by exhortation is the last refuge of the incompetent manager.

- *Planning*: set up planning procedures which involve people in different units and at different levels in jointly formulating policies and preparing plans.
- *Management information*: install management information systems which help to identify areas where joint action is required.

Teamwork

Every manager should be aware that his job is as much about getting people to work well together – team building – as it is about motivating individual members of his staff. Teamwork will be improved if the various measures to achieve integration mentioned above are used. But you as a manager have an important role to play.

Aim

Your aim should be to build a team which is cohesive, self-supporting and knows where it is going. The main features of such a team will be:

1. The task of the group is well understood and accepted by its members. They will have been involved in discussing the task from time to time in a way which enables them to commit themselves to its achievement.
2. Clear group assignments are made and accepted.
3. There is a fair amount of discussion in which everyone participates, but it remains pertinent to the task of the group.
4. Members listen to each other. People feel free to express their views. Every idea is given a hearing.
5. There is disagreement, but it is open and resolved by discussion rather than domination.
6. Criticism is frank, but it is about the work being done and is not personal.
7. The atmosphere tends to be informal.
8. The leader of the group does not over-dominate it, nor does the group defer unduly to him.

Team building methods

To build an effective team you should:

1. Know where you want them to go.
2. Know how they are going to get there.
3. Know what you expect each member of the team to achieve.
4. Know what you are doing.
5. Encourage participation in agreeing objectives and targets.
6. Group related tasks together so that group members know that they can make their jobs easier by co-operating with others.
7. Rotate jobs within groups so that team members identify with the team rather than with their own jobs.
8. Ensure that communications flow freely in and between groups.

Managing conflict

Conflict will happen in your organization. In fact, it is a good thing if it does. Conflict is healthy; bland agreement probably means that the issues have not been thoroughly debated. There is not necessarily one right way of doing anything and it is just as well that different approaches are brought out into the open and resolved. But conflict becomes counter-productive when it is based on personality clashes, or when it is treated as something unpleasant which ought to go away, rather than as a problem to be 'worked through'.

Resolving conflict

There are three ways of resolving conflict:

1. *Peaceful co-existence*: the aim here is to smooth out differences and emphasize the common ground. People are encouraged to learn to live together; there is a good deal of information, contact and exchange of views, and individuals move freely between groups (eg between headquarters and the field, or between sales and manufacturing).

   This is a pleasant ideal, but it may not be practicable in many situations. There is much evidence that conflict is not necessarily resolved by grouping people together. Improved communications and techniques such as team briefing may appear to be good ideas, but are useless if management has nothing to say that people want to hear. There is also the danger that the real issues, submerged for the moment in an atmosphere of superficial *bonhomie*, will surface again at a later date.
2. *Compromise*: the issue is resolved by negotiation or bargaining and neither party wins or loses. This concept of splitting the difference is essentially pessimistic. Agreements only accommodate differences; real issues are not likely to be solved.
3. *Problem solving*: an attempt is made to find a genuine solution to

the problem rather than just accommodating different points of view. This is where the apparent paradox of 'creative conflict' comes in. Conflict situations can be used to advantage to create better solutions.

If solutions are to be developed by problem solving, they have to be generated by those who share the responsibility for seeing that the solutions work. The sequence of actions is: first, those concerned work to define the problem and agree on the objectives to be attained in reaching a solution; second, the group develops alternative solutions and debates their merits; third, agreement is reached on the preferred course of action and how it should be implemented.

Managing change

Change is always with us but it is not always welcome. It has to be managed.

Resistance to change

Resistance to change is natural. It arises because of:

- *Habit*: once a habit has been established it provides comfort and satisfaction.
- *Conformity*: people like to conform to customary and expected ways of behaving. Anything new is potentially disruptive.
- *Threat*: change within organizations may provide a threat. People may be worried because they see change as likely to do them more harm than good. They perceive a possible loss of money, security or status.
- *Misunderstanding*: people often misunderstand the implications of change and believe that it will cost them more than they will gain.
- *Different perceptions*: people may assess the situation differently from their managers and concentrate on the costs rather than the benefits.

Overcoming resistance to change

Managing change is a matter of overcoming resistance. You will be successful in doing this if you ensure that:

- Those affected by change feel that they can accept the project as their own, not one imposed upon them by outsiders.
- The change has the wholehearted support of management.
- The change accords with well-established values.

- The change is seen as reducing rather than increasing present burdens.
- The change offers the kind of new experience which interests participants.
- Participants feel that their autonomy and security are not threatened.
- Participants have jointly diagnosed the problems.
- The change has been agreed by group decisions.
- Those advocating change understand the feelings and fears of those affected and take steps to relieve unnecessary fears.
- It is recognized that new ideas are likely to be misinterpreted and ample provision is made for discussion of reactions to proposals, to ensure complete understanding of them.

Achieving commitment

The need

Organizations exist to reach their objectives by getting the right work done. Clearly, this is most likely to take place if you obtain the maximum degree of commitment from your staff.

Some people, with a built-in drive for making things happen, will be fully committed. All you need to do with these achievers is to point them in the right direction, give them sufficient scope, and off they will go. But a large proportion will need encouragement, some more than others.

Factors affecting commitment

Two factors affect commitment:

1. *Environment*: the organization's culture and values will encourage or discourage achievers.
2. *Individual*: an individual's degree of commitment will be affected by the way in which he is led and motivated.

Increasing commitment

The following are the steps you can take to increase commitment:

1. *Motivation*: introduce programmes for increasing motivation (see Chapter 5).
2. *Leadership*: exercise more effective leadership (see Chapter 6).
3. *Identification*: develop identification with the company and its values by means of:
   - *communications*: introduce continuous programmes of communication which are led from the top and involve all key managers in regular contact with individuals and groups, where

the message can be presented and discussed in a face-to-face setting (see Chapter 7);

- *participation*: get employees involved in decision making on matters that affect them, so that they can get closer to the issues and the company itself (see Chapter 14);
- *employees' ideas*: give employees the opportunity to contribute and therefore 'own' ideas about how productivity, quality and any other areas of company activity can be improved, through such approaches as quality circles (see Chapter 14);
- *training*: use training programmes to present the values of the company, get people involved in groups to promote understanding of the company and each other, and develop the right attitudes and skills in such matters as quality and service to customers (see Chapter 9);
- *profit sharing*: give employees a financial stake in the company and relate their rewards to improvements in company performance (see Chapter 12).

4. *Accountable management*: a system of accountable management obtains commitment by ensuring that people know what they have to achieve and are aware of how their performance will be measured against agreed targets and standards. The principle behind the system is the same as that of management by objectives, but it avoids the mounds of paperwork and the rigid procedures that destroyed the credibility of many M by O schemes. And it concentrates on the job in hand rather than preparing woolly proposals for long-term management development into a future that may never happen. The use of the concept of accountable management in performance appraisal is described in Chapter 10.

5. *The reward system*: introduce a reward system which, as far as possible, relates pay to individual performance as assessed in a system of accountable management or measured in payment by results schemes (see Chapter 12).

6. *Caring*: caring means treating employees as human beings, not machines. They are looked after by the company in sickness, distress and on retirement. Amenities such as restaurants and rest rooms are provided by the company to promote their well-being. Within the limitations imposed by the type of work, the environment is pleasant; it is certainly conducive to health and safety. Social and sporting activities are encouraged and supported and facilities are provided.

Action in each of these areas would be aimed to make people feel the company is worth working for and to generate a spirit of 'togetherness' (especially with regard to sport and social facilities).

There is, however, a limit to their effectiveness. They can be taken for granted. Magnificent sports facilities can be supported only by a few enthusiasts.

Of course, you should be concerned about your employees' health and safety and do everything you can to provide a pleasant working environment, but you can go too far with welfare. Is it really the role of the company to look after just about every aspect of an employee's life? The Japanese may have tendencies in that direction, but that is another culture. A 'caring' approach, together with the more specific actions referred to earlier will help to achieve commitment, but its impact may be limited.

5. Motivating Human Resources

Motivating human resources (MHR) is very much concerned with maintaining corporate cultures and values which will be conducive to high performance. The organizational aspects of this requirement were considered in earlier chapters. But to achieve 'mutuality', in the sense of a shared interest in success, it is also necessary to consider what you can do to encourage individuals and groups of people to give of their best in a way which will further the interests of the organization, as well as their own. This means looking at the processes of motivation and leadership, discussed in the next two chapters.

WHAT IS MOTIVATION?

A motive is something which initiates movement; motivation is about what makes people act or behave in certain ways. To motivate people is to point them in a certain direction and take whatever steps are required to ensure that they get there. To be motivated is either to want to go somewhere of one's own volition, or to be encouraged by whatever means are available to get going purposefully and to achieve success on arrival.

Motivation comes in two basic forms:

1. *Extrinsic motivation*: what you do to or for people to motivate them.
2. *Intrinsic motivation*: the self-generated factors which influence people to behave in particular ways or to move in particular directions.

In practice, these two forms are inextricably linked, as shown in Figure 5.1. What you do to or for people will affect their self-motivation. The degree to which people are self-motivated and the directions that they set themselves will inevitably affect the extent to which you can influence them.

Put another way, motivation is about what makes people tick; to

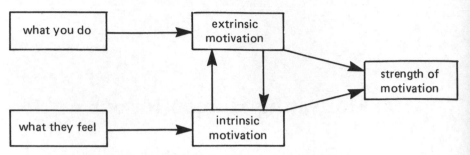

Figure 5.1 *Influences on motivation*

motivate is to ensure that people tick in the way you want them to – but what *you* want them to do and what *they* want to do will not necessarily coincide. The aim of motivation is to achieve a sense of common purpose by ensuring that, so far as possible, the wants and needs of the organization and the wants and needs of its members are in harmony.

Motivation, however, is a complex process. The biggest mistake you can make as a manager is to believe that there is a simplistic answer to motivating people. To motivate effectively you need to:

- Understand the basic process of motivation, the need – goal – action model and the influences of experience and expectations.
- Know about the factors affecting motivation – the pattern of needs that initiates drives towards goals and the circumstances in which needs are satisfied or unsatisfied.
- Appreciate that motivation is not just a matter of forking out more cash.
- Appreciate also that motivation cannot be achieved simply by creating feelings of satisfaction – too much of that can breed complacency and inertia.
- Understand, in the light of all these factors, the complex relationship between motivation and performance.

When, and only when, you have taken all this on board, will you be ready to motivate by using motivating techniques which are appropriate to the needs of the situation and of the people involved in it.

THE PROCESS OF MOTIVATION

The process of motivation is initiated by someone recognizing – consciously or unconsciously – an unsatisfied need. A goal is then established which, it is thought, will satisfy that need, and a course of action is determined that will lead towards the attainment of the goal and, therefore, the satisfaction of the need. This process is illustrated in Figure 5.2.

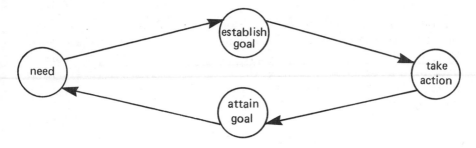

Figure 5.2 *The process of motivation*

The strength of motivation is influenced by two things: experience and expectations.

The influence of experience

As experience is gained in taking action to satisfy needs, people perceive that certain actions help to achieve their goals while others are less successful. Some actions bring rewards, others result in failure or even punishment. The rewards act as positive incentives and reinforce the successful behaviour, which is repeated the next time a similar need emerges. The more powerful, obvious and frequent the reinforcement, the more likely it is that behaviour will be repeated until, eventually, it becomes a more or less unconscious reaction to an event. Conversely, failures or punishments suggest that it is necessary to seek alternative means of achieving goals. This is sometimes called the law of effect.

The degree to which experience shapes future behaviour depends on the extent to which someone is able to recognize the resemblance between the previous situation and the one that now confronts him. Perceptive ability varies between people, as does the ability to identify correlations between events. For these reasons, some people are better at learning from experience than others, just as some people are more easily motivated than others.

The existence of this pressure from the past is, of course, an explanation of why people resist change. If something has worked well for an individual in the past, why should he exchange it for something that might not work well in the future? Even if things have not been so good, a change might make them worse. There is a tendency for people to expect the worst, which is why expectations also have a major influence on the process of motivation.

The influence of expectations

Experience may suggest to you that what has happened in the past will happen in the future; but you may not be sure, particularly in changing or turbulent conditions - and these are endemic in most organizations. People will only act if they have a reasonable belief that their actions will lead to desired goals. Even if their goals are valued, they will not necessarily aim for them if they don't think the ball has any chance of getting into the net.

The strength of expectations may indeed be based on past experiences (reinforcement), but individuals are frequently presented with new situations - a change in job, payment systems or working conditions imposed by management - where past experience is an inadequate guide to the implications of the change. In these circumstances motivation may be reduced.

Motivation is only likely when a clearly perceived and usable relationship exists between performance and outcome, and the outcome is seen as satisfying needs. This explains why an incentive scheme only works if the link between effort and reward is clear and the value of the reward is worth the effort.

FACTORS AFFECTING MOTIVATION

Needs

The process of motivation is started by the identification of a need. One of the main reasons for the complexity of this process is that, because individuals differ so much, it is impossible to produce a universal law which will predict how people will behave in particular circumstances.

Attempts have, however, been made to classify needs and to describe how they operate. The most famous of these was formulated by Abraham Maslow: he suggested that there are five major need categories which apply to people in general, starting from the fundamental physiological needs and leading through a hierarchy to the need for self-fulfilment, the highest need of all. Maslow's hierarchy is as follows:

1. *Physiological*: the need for food, drink and the other things essential for survival.
2. *Safety*: the need for protection against danger and the deprivation of physiological needs.
3. *Social*: the need for love, affection and to be accepted as belonging to a social group.
4. *Esteem*: the need to have a stable and high evaluation of oneself (self-esteem) and to have the respect of others (prestige). This need embraces the important desires for adequacy, achievement, reputation and status.

5. *Self-fulfilment*: the need to develop potentialities and skills, to become what one believes one is capable of becoming (self-actualization).

This hierarchy can be represented as a pyramid of needs as shown in Figure 5.3. The basis of Maslow's theory about how these needs operate is that man is a 'wanting animal'. Only an unsatisfied need can motivate behaviour and the dominant need is the prime motivator of behaviour. As a lower need is satisfied the next highest becomes dominant and the individual's attention is turned to satisfying this higher need, although the need for self-fulfilment can never be satisfied. The lower needs still exist, however, and individuals constantly return to previously satisfied needs.

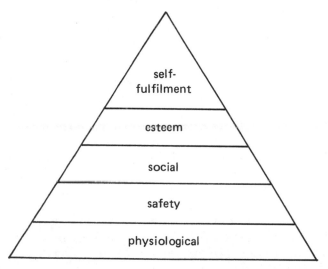

Figure 5.3 *Maslow's hierarchy of needs*

The 'ERG' model of needs was developed by Alderfer in an attempt to make the Maslow hierarchy more meaningful. The three basic needs are:

1. *Existence*: the need for food, shelter and money. These are not insatiable and individuals have a certain degree of satisfaction they regard as enough.
2. *Relatedness*: the need for the mutual sharing of thoughts and feelings with other people.
3. Growth: the need to develop whatever abilities and capacities the individual feels are most important to him or her.

An alternative way of classifying the needs that motivate managers was developed by David McClelland. He identified three needs as being important:

1. *The need for achievement*, defined as the need for competitive success.
2. *The need for affiliation*, defined as the need for warm, friendly relationships with others.
3. *The need for power*, defined as the need to control or influence others.

Different managers have different levels of these needs. Some have a greater need for achievement, others a stronger need for affiliation, and still others a stronger need for power. The most rounded managers have well-developed needs for achievement, but success in a competitive world often springs from an urge to achieve power.

Circumstances leading to satisfaction of needs

If you are concerned about motivating people – and if you are a manager you must be – then you have to ask yourself: 'Given these classifications of needs, what are the circumstances that will lead to their satisfaction and, presumably, improved performance, or at least willingness to stay on the job?'

One way of answering this question is to establish which of the features in working life are likely to lead to the satisfaction of needs or dissatisfaction. The most persuasive solution was provided by Saul Herzberg, whose research resulted in his formulation of the two-factor model of satisfiers and dissatisfiers. The research was conducted by asking a number of people to describe events at work which made them feel satisfied or dissatisfied. These were classified by Herzberg as those events most likely to cause lasting satisfaction and those which cause dissatisfaction.

The 'satisfiers' in order of the frequency with which they were mentioned were achievement, recognition, the work itself, responsibility and advancement. In terms of the length of time feelings about the events lasted, however, responsibility was the key factor. The 'dissatisfiers' in order of frequency were company policy and administration, technical supervision, salary, relationships with supervision, and working conditions.

As Herzberg commented, the group of satisfying factors revolve round the need to develop in one's own occupation as a source of personal growth. The factors causing dissatisfaction act as an essential base to the first and are associated with fair treatment in compensation, supervision, working conditions and administrative practices. Neglecting this group can certainly cause dissatisfaction but will not necessarily cause satisfaction. Herzberg calls them the 'hygiene factors' because they provide the basis for good health but do not guarantee it in themselves. Lasting satisfaction can only be provided by fostering the first group of factors. The message is, in the words of the old Bing Crosby song, 'accentuate the positive and eliminate the negative'.

SATISFACTION AND MOTIVATION

The ideas of Herzberg and others seem to suggest that your aim should be to create satisfying conditions and remove those causing dissatisfaction. This seems reasonable, but can you be certain that a satisfied worker is necessarily a productive worker?

A lot of research has been carried out on this subject and has failed to prove that there is an inevitable correlation between satisfaction and performance. In fact, common sense suggests that a bovine self-satisfied worker may be content to do no more than stay with the firm doing the minimum amount of work required to keep him employed. On the other hand, a dissatisfied worker could be motivated to do much better in order to improve his lot – as long as he believes that harder work will get him somewhere. Increases in job satisfaction may therefore reduce staff turnover, absenteeism and grievances, but may not necessarily result in increases in productivity. Satisfaction and performance are often related, but the precise effect on one another depends on the working situation and the people in it. People are best motivated when they have something to strive for. A measure of dissatisfaction and a desire for more achievement or power may be the best motivator for some people. It will all depend on the people concerned and the environment in which they are working.

THE RELATIONSHIP BETWEEN MOTIVATION AND PERFORMANCE

There may be some doubts about the link between satisfaction and motivation but, almost by definition, it would seem that the link between motivation and performance is a positive one: increased motivation results in more effort and improved performance. It can be argued, however, that while high motivation will produce better performance, improvements in performance will increase motivation because of the resulting sense of achievement. It is something of a chicken and egg situation as illustrated in Figure 5.4.

But there is even more to it than that. There are two qualifications to the simple view that high motivation gets results: first the influence of ability; and second, the effects of too much motivation.

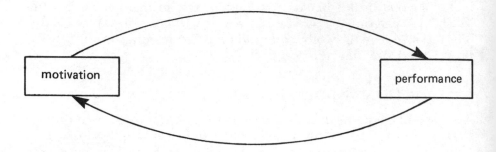

Figure 5.4 *Relationship between motivation and performance*

Motivation and ability

However keen someone is to do something, he will not be able to do it unless he has the required abilities. The level of ability will affect not only performance but also job satisfaction and the desire to stay on the job. The relationships concerned are illustrated in Figure 5.5. The implication is that it is just as necessary to take steps to improve ability by means of good selection and training as it is to pay attention to motivation by using the extrinsic and intrinsic factors that affect it.

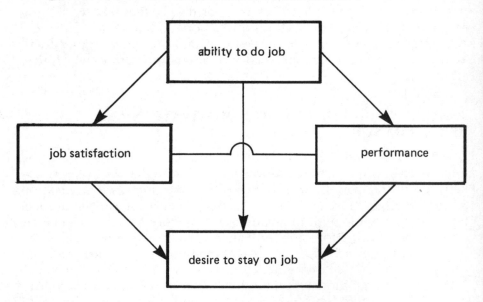

Figure 5.5 *Motivation relationships*

Effects of high motivation

Motivation implies pressure – to move forward, to do more – but pressure can induce stress; too much motivation may equal too much stress, and performance can suffer. The limit to how much people can be motivated depends upon the strength of their needs and their ability to cope with pressure.

MOTIVATION MODELS

The best way to summarize and use the various concepts of motivation discussed in this chapter is to develop motivation models. You have a choice about which model to adopt. Some perhaps over-simplify the issues, while you may feel that others over-complicate them. There is no one model that applies to everyone in every circumstance, although the more complex ones may cover a greater range of eventualities. The various models are discussed below.

The rational man model

According to this view, people are motivated by a combination of financial rewards, and punishments, as shown in Figure 5.6. This is the carrot and stick approach. Herzberg described the management technique which relies on sanctions to get results as KITA (kick in the arse).

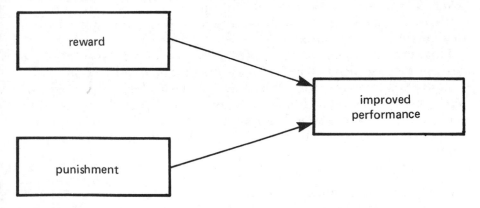

Figure 5.6 *The rational motivation model*

For some people and in some circumstances this approach works; but the effects may only be short-term, and its failure to recognize that there are other human needs means that its exclusive use in all situations can create longer-term damage.

The human relations model

This model was developed by the human relations school of researchers and writers on management, led by Elton Mayo. They demonstrated through research that formal incentive schemes often did not work, either because they could be manipulated or even sabotaged by

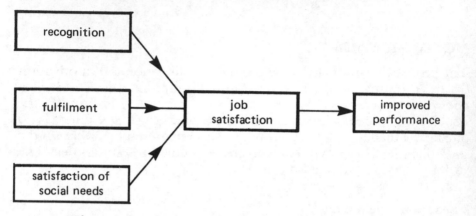

Figure 5.7 *The human relations model of motivation*

employees acting individually or together, or because they did not appeal to other than fundamental needs. They suggested that productivity was directly related to job satisfaction, which was derived more from intrinsic factors such as recognition, a sense of fulfilment and satisfaction of social needs, than extrinsic factors such as pay and working conditions. Figure 5.7 shows this relationship.

This approach ignores the powerful impact of the directly motivating extrinsic factors, such as pay. It also assumes that job satisfaction results in improved performance, which, as we have already seen, is not necessarily the case. The human relations model provides a necessary modification to the crude KITA approach, but being nice to people is not enough. The assumption that a contented person is a productive person is naive.

The self-actualizing model

The self-actualizing model was developed by Maslow and Herzberg on the basis of their analysis of needs and their belief that the most important of these needs, from the point of view of longer-term motivation, were those concerned with self-fulfilment or actualization. These needs are intrinsic to people and are not subject to the external control system.

Other major influences on this school were Douglas McGregor, who pointed out that, 'people will exercise self-direction and self-control in the achievement of organizational objectives to the degree that they are committed to those objectives', and Chris Argyris, who sees each individual as having a potential that the organization and he can jointly realize to their mutual benefit.

The school of behavioural scientists who developed this model also made the distinction between the extrinsic and intrinsic motivating factors mentioned earlier in this chapter. Their philosophy is that it is the intrinsic factors that really count.

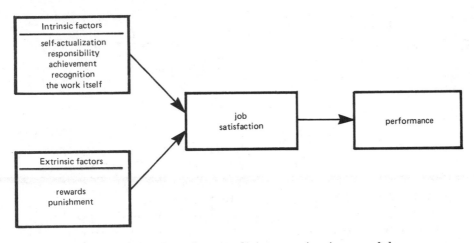

Figure 5.8 *The self-actualizing motivation model*

The self-actualizing model is illustrated in Figure 5.8. The difficulty with this model is that it probably underestimates the role of money as a motivator. It can be argued that money must be the prime motivator because it is the means of satisfying so many needs, including recognition, achievement, status, and self-fulfilment. The model also fails to cater for the complex relationship between job satisfaction and performance and the influence of expectations.

The complex model

None of the models described so far is wrong; their only fault is that they over-simplify. Motivation is a complicated affair: first, because people are complicated, with a multitude of needs and expectations; second, because the situations in which people work vary and affect motivation patterns in different ways; and third, because these people and situations are in a constant state of change. The models make the assumption that

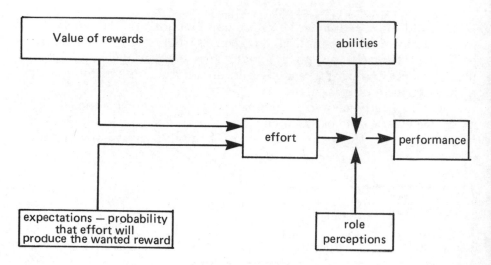

Figure 5.9 *Complex motivation model*

satisfaction increases motivation, which cannot be sustained, and they do not take sufficient account of expectations, ability levels, the perceived value of the reward and what may be called role perception – feelings about what the individual wants to do or thinks he is required to.

The model illustrated in Figure 5.9, based on one developed by two American researchers, Lawler and Porter, attempts to describe these complex interrelationships. This model identifies two prime factors which determine the effort a person puts into a job:

1. The value of the rewards to the individual in so far as they are likely to satisfy his needs.
2. The expectation that the effort he makes will result in the reward he wants.

But effort is not enough. It has to be effective effort if it is to produce the desired performance. The two additional variables to effort which affect motivation are:

1. *Ability*: individual characteristics such as intelligence, manual skills, know-how.
2. *Role perception*: the individual's feelings about his job. These are good from the point of view of the organization if what the individual wants to do is what the organization would like him to. This, fundamentally, is the result you need to achieve.

MOTIVATION TECHNIQUES

The need to analyse

Motivation is, or should be, an analytical process. It is based on appreciation of the process of motivation and the models described above, and an understanding of the needs of the organization and the people in it, in relation to the demands made by the environment on both the organization and its members. The interrelationship between these factors is shown in Figure 5.10.

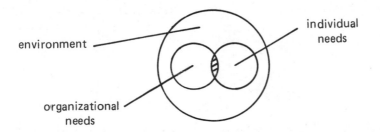

Figure 5.10 *Interrelationships between organizational and individual needs and the environment*

Organizational and individual needs overlap within the working environment. The aim is to optimize the area of overlap between the two needs circles; they can never coincide. There will always be occasions when the organization is forced to do something which will damage the interests of one or more of its members. At the same time, individuals must and should have a high proportion of their needs satisfied out of work. Sadly, however, what frequently happens is that because individuals do not get the opportunity to satisfy their needs at work, they take their talents elsewhere, possibly to another job but frequently to outside interests. Many frustrated managers have directed their managerial skills to politics and excelled there, to the surprise of their bosses.

Your analysis should therefore cover:

1. *The environment in which your company operates*: the threats it is facing, the opportunities available to it, the impact of external influences and internal developments on the needs of the company and its employees.
2. *Organizational needs*: your corporate and organization development plans and your human resource plans should tell you where you are going, what you want people to do and what sort of people you want to do it.
3. *Individual needs*: this is the key analytical area, but it is also the

most difficult one. It is too easy to make generalizations about what people want, based on our own experience and observations; but these generalizations can err. The complex nature of the motivational process described earlier in this chapter guarantees mistakes when judging what individuals or groups of employees need or want. One of the problems is that so many needs can operate at so many different levels to which are attached a wide variety of goals. To some people, security is all they want, some only need prestige and esteem, while others aim for self-fulfilment. Each of these needs can be satisfied in different ways inside and outside work, and there are a number of alternative actions which will achieve desired goals. This complicated set-up is illustrated in Figure 5.11.

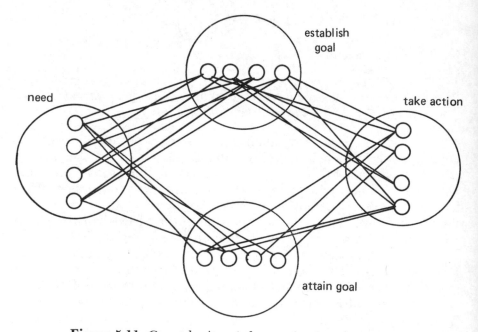

Figure 5.11 *Complexity of the motivational process*

A futher difficulty in analysing individual needs is that all you observe is behaviour – actions taken to achieve goals. The needs that motivate that behaviour remain hidden. A certain amount of generalization is therefore inevitable. You can, however, avoid the worst pitfalls by not jumping to conclusions. If a group of employees or an individual act in a certain way, remember the various needs that may have prompted them, as listed earlier in this chapter, and try to find out what is really motivating or bugging them. Think about what has been going on and how it might have affected people. Talk to them, ask around. If you want to be more scientific, commission an attitude survey which will elicit views from employees about the company. Some firms, such as IBM, conduct them regularly to identify changes and trends in attitudes and modify their personnel policies or practices accordingly.

Armed with this information and your knowledge of the processes involved you are in a position to develop motivation strategies, as discussed in the next section.

MOTIVATION STRATEGIES

Simplistic approaches

There are three basic approaches which have been advocated by motivation experts. Each has its merits, but because they are often put forward as the only answer to all your motivation problems, they are essentially simplistic. The three approaches are:

1. *Carrot and stick*: people work for rewards. They will work hard if you pay them well and will work harder if you pay them more. If they do not perform satisfactorily, then you punish them.
2. *Motivate through the work itself*: give people fulfilling work and their level of job satisfaction, and therefore performance, will be high.
3. *The one-minute manager system*: set goals with your subordinates and give them positive feedback when they do something right and negative feedback when they do something wrong.

Managers, according to their inclinations, take up these nostrums because they seem easy, a quick fix in a complex world. There is nothing wrong with any one of them – for the right people, in the right place and at the right time – but the complexity of the process of motivation and the infinitely varying demands made by different situations do not admit any 'quick fixes'. You have to develop your motivation strategy on the basis of your analysis of the situation and incorporate in it the mix of techniques that are appropriate to that situation.

Motivation methods

The methods of motivation available to you are to:

1. Use money as a reward and an incentive.

2. Spell out requirements.
3. Develop commitment.
4. Motivate through the work itself.
5. Reward and recognize achievement.
6. Exercise leadership.
7. Build up teamwork.
8. Train and develop people.
9. Eliminate the negatives.

Each of these methods is discussed below.

Money

Money, in the form of pay or some other sort of remuneration, is the most obvious extrinsic reward. Money provides the carrot which most, if not all, people want.

Doubts have been cast on the effectiveness of money by Herzberg because while the lack of it can cause dissatisfaction, its provision does not result in lasting satisfaction. There is something in this, especially for people on fixed salaries or rates of pay who do not benefit directly from an incentive scheme. They may feel good when they get an increase – apart from the extra money, it is about as tangible a form of recognition as you can find – but this feeling of euphoria can rapidly die away. Other dissatisfactions from Herzberg's list of hygiene factors, such as working conditions or the quality of management, loom larger in their minds, or they fail to get the satisfaction they need from the work itself.

Nevertheless, money provides the means to achieve a number of different ends. It is a powerful force because it is linked directly or indirectly to the satisfaction of many needs. In Maslow's hierarchy, it clearly satisfies the basic needs for survival and security, if it is coming in regularly. It can also satisfy the need for self-esteem (as noted above, it is a visible mark of appreciation) and status – money can set you in a grade apart from your fellows and can buy you things they can't to build up your prestige. Money satisfies the less desirable but still prevalent drives of acquisitiveness and cupidity.

Money may in itself have no intrinsic meaning, but it acquires significant motivating power because it comes to symbolize so many intangible goals. It acts as a symbol in different ways for different people, and for the same person at different times.

Research carried out by Ashridge College among managers in a large British company revealed that when asked to rate the importance of a list of tangible and intangible rewards, the largest group (25 per cent) was mainly interested in material reward, expressed in money, fringe benefits and opportunities for promotion. This group was younger and potentially more mobile than the two next largest groups, who were interested in status and prestige (19 per cent) or a comfortable secure life among friends (18 per cent). Money, of course, appeals to 'stars' – the young upwardly mobile professionals – and they are important to any organization. But in paying attention to their needs you should not neglect the journeyman and solid citizens upon whom you rely to get most of the more boring work done.

Another piece of research carried out by Goldthorpe among 'affluent' skilled and semi-skilled workers, revealed that the workers were motivated in their choice of employer by the extrinsic factors of pay and, to a lesser extent, security. They wanted to increase their power as consumers and their domestic standard of living, rather than satisfy themselves as producers or by the degree of fulfilment they got from work.

People certainly want money and, just as certainly, you have to pay the right amount to get and keep them in most organizations. The only exceptions are the relatively few cases where the intrinsic attraction of the work itself overrides financial considerations. The effectiveness of money as a means of improving performance and increasing productivity, however, depends upon it being seen as a reasonably sure means of achieving a goal. Its force will depend on two factors: first, the strength of the need; and second, the degree to which a person is confident that his behaviour will earn the money he wants to satisfy the need, ie his expectations about the likelihood of his effort being adequately rewarded.

Money can therefore provide positive motivation in the right circumstances, but Herzberg is correct in pointing out that pay systems can demotivate. Another researcher in this area was Elliott Jaques, who emphasized the need for such systems to be perceived as being fair and equitable. In other words, the reward should be clearly related to effort or level of responsibility and people should not receive less money than they deserve compared with their fellow workers. Jaques called this the 'felt-fair' principle.

To use money effectively as a motivator and to avoid it acting as a demotivator you need to:

- Pay competitive rates to attract and retain people.
- Provide the rate for the job which must reflect the value of the work to the company and be paid fairly and equitably.
- Relate pay to performance or results wherever possible, thus providing a direct incentive.

Remember that incentive or bonus schemes only work as motivators if it is felt that: 1) the reward is worth having in relation to the effort; 2) the reward is commensurate with the effort; and 3) the worker can confidently expect that his effort will be followed by the reward – quickly and consistently.

Spell out requirements

Motivation is not simply a matter of providing rewards and incentives. People have to know what they are expected to do and what will happen to them if they do not do it. They need to be clear about their roles, the objectives they have to achieve and the required standards of performance and behaviour. They can be made aware of the rewards in the shape of money, advancement or improved status that will result from compliance with these expectations (the carrot); but they must be equally aware of the sanctions that will be applied if they fail (the stick).

Motivation, as has already been said, is not just about being nice to people. You have every right to be demanding, as long as you reward people adequately if they meet your demands; and they will respect you for it. Equally, you have the right to take corrective action if they do not fulfil your requirements; again, you will be respected for doing this as long as you have acted fairly and those concerned are quite clear about what to expect.

Develop commitment

You should do whatever you can to increase commitment to and identification with the organization. Your aim should be to integrate so far as possible the needs of the organization with those of the individual, so that the latter believes that if the organization thrives with his help, he will thrive too. You have also to appeal to the 'What's in it for me?' reaction. People may work hard if they believe in the mission of the company and can identify with its values, aims and activities; they will work even harder if they feel that achieving the results the company wants does something for them too.

Methods of increasing commitment and identification through organization development were discussed in Chapter 4. They can be furthered by the other motivational methods referred to below, and by the approaches to leadership and 'getting it across to people' through better communications and involvement, covered in the next two chapters.

Motivating through the work itself

Given an equitable and competitive pay structure which, so far as possible, offers effective financial incentives, you can increase identification and provide for long-lasting motivation by developing an intrinsic reward system. Intrinsic rewards are contained in the content of the job and give satisfaction by enabling people to feel a sense of accomplishment, to express and use their abilities, and to exercise their own decision-making powers. Motivation through the work itself is mainly a matter of job design and job enrichment as described in Chapter 3.

Reward and recognize achievement

Your pay system can be geared to providing appropriate rewards for achievement, but you can also reward people by giving them more responsibility (an intrinsic reward) as well as opportunities for promotion and increased status (extrinsic rewards). Tangible rewards are best, as long as they have been earned and people appreciate that fact. Praise for work well done is, however, an important motivator although, again, it must be earned. It is devalued if it is given to liberally.

Exercise leadership

Leadership plays a key role in motivation. It promotes commitment and identification, as mentioned above, but it also provides a sense of direction. It can clarify roles and objectives, develop a sense of purpose and foster team spirit. Inspirational leadership from charismatic figures who get everyone to accept what are sometimes called 'superordinate goals' – ie aims above and beyond the call of duty – can be appropriate in some circumstances, for example in crises. But the cool, quiet, restrained leader who carries people with him just because he clearly knows where he is going and how he is going to get there – with the help of his team – can be equally effective in the appropriate situation.

Build up teamwork

A cohesive team will carry all its members along with it. Enthusiasm is infectious, so if you can engender enthusiasm for the task in your team, you are are much more likely to get everyone going your way. You should bear in mind, however, that teams can work against you. Many an incentive scheme has been ruined by workers who have restricted earning levels and ganged up against rate busters because they felt that otherwise, management would tighten up rates. Team-building activities, as discussed in Chapter 3 and also in the next chapter, aim to achieve positive cohesion and overcome the negative influences that groups can exert.

Train and develop people

Systematic training and development programmes, as described in Chapter 13, will provide motivation by giving people the opportunity to enhance their skills and to achieve positions of greater responsibility. Sending someone away on a course can be a good way of showing him that he is valued. Company training programmes, especially residential ones, can help to improve the identification with the organization of those attending.

Eliminate the negatives
So far, we have accentuated the positive aids to motivation. There are, however, the negative dissatisfiers as listed by Herzberg (the hygiene factors) which you must do your best to minimize. An inequitable pay structure, as referred to earlier, is one of them; poor working conditions, inadequate supervision and unduly restrictive or bureaucratic practices are others. You will never prevent people grousing about these, but you can at least reduce the scope for legitimate grumbles.

Putting the motivation package together

All the methods of motivation that have been described can and should be used. However, the mix will depend on the individual concerned and the requirements of the organization. Although carrot and stick techniques are deplored by some human relations experts, they do work, and used judiciously, they have to form part of the motivation programme. However, they do not work equally well in all circumstances and their impact may be limited, bearing in mind that they do not satisfy any of the intrinsic needs which are powerful long-term motivators. It is important to cater for these needs in your programme by motivating through the work itself. It is equally important to encourage the integration of the needs of the individuals with those of the organization by increasing identification and by training. Finally, you should do what you can to mitigate the demotivating factors.

6. Leadership

WHAT IS LEADERSHIP?

Leadership is getting things done through people – when there is an objective to be achieved, or a task to be carried out and when more than one person is needed to do it. All managers are by definition leaders, in that they can only do what they have to do with the support of their team, who must be inspired or persuaded to follow them. Leadership is therefore about encouraging and inspiring individuals and teams to give their best to achieve a desired result.

Leadership plays a key role in human resource management. As was noted in Chapter 2, the achievement of excellence in business and management depends largely on the ability of the leader to convey his vision, enthusiasm and sense of purpose to his team.

Leadership is required because someone has to point the way and that same person has to ensure that everyone concerned gets there. Organizational effectiveness depends on the quality of leadership.

OBJECTIVES OF A LEADER

The overall aim of a leader is to achieve the task with the help of his group and to meet this aim, the leader has three main objectives:

1. To gain the commitment and co-operation of his team.
2. To get the group into action to achieve agreed objectives.
3. To make the best use of the skills, energies and talents of the team.

A leader's aim is to get people to do what he wants by obtaining willing co-operation, not grudging submission. He must also build up the morale of his group, which will be high when the group is productive and the people in it work well together. They don't need to feel comfortable – in fact, they will often be under pressure to do more than they would if left to their own devices – but they will feel that they are achieving something worthwhile together and gain satisfaction from that.

HOW ARE OBJECTIVES ACHIEVED?

The most familiar saying about leadership is that, 'Leaders are born, not made'. Like all clichés there is some truth in it, although it should not be taken literally. There are many successful leaders around who demonstrated their abilities at an early age and have never looked back since. They have natural talents, and although they may not have actually been born with them, these talents have been fostered by their early upbringing and experiences at school, university or in the armed forces. Their 'charisma', inspirational qualities and ways of handling people appear to combine together to produce a person about whom everyone says, 'He's a natural leader'. It may seem effortless, but of course it isn't. As Lao Tzu wrote in the 6th century BC: 'The great rulers – the people do not notice their existence.'

Effective leaders start with some natural talents, and then they build on them. They are good at observing how to do it and how not to do it. They learn from their experience and they keep on learning. It cannot be said of one of them that: 'Here is a man whose 20 years' experience is one year's experience repeated 20 times.' The good leaders take pains to analyse their successes and failures and learn from them.

Given certain natural leadership abilities, how do you improve them? By practice of course, but also by observation and analysis of yourself as well as of others. The rest of this chapter aims to help you by providing an analytical framework for this purpose. This will be done by answering three key questions about leadership:

1. What is a leader?
2. What do leaders do?
3. How do leaders do it?

It will then be possible to summarize the ways in which leadership effectiveness can be maximized.

WHAT IS A LEADER?

There are many answers to this question. According to the American management writers, Warren Bennis and Burt Vanus, about 250 definitions have been produced by writers on leadership. Not one of them achieved the necessary combination of clarity and completeness.

Most attempts to define what a leader is concentrate on the qualities required, the factors influencing success, the personality traits of successful leaders, or the types of leader that exist. Each of these approaches to defining a leader will be considered in this section. All of them look at the leader from his or the organization's point of view but, by definition, leaders have followers and further insight into what leaders are can be gained by considering them from the standpoint of their subordinates.

Leadership qualities

The British expert on leadership, John Adair, quoted the following ranking of the 12 attributes rated most valuable at the top level of management by successful chief executives:

1. Decisiveness.
2. Leadership.
3. Integrity.
4. Enthusiasm.
5. Imagination.
6. Willingness to work hard.
7. Analytical ability.
8. Understanding of others.
9. Ability to spot opportunities.
10. Ability to meet unpleasant situations.
11. Ability to adapt quickly to change.
12. Willingness to take risks.

One of the problems with this sort of list is that the qualities are often difficult to define. John Adair pointed out that another survey of 75 top executives revealed that the definition of dependability included 147 different concepts.

Another difficulty is that the qualities may have to be used in different ways in different circumstances and they need to be deployed judiciously. For example, consistency is a good thing if it means that people know where they stand, don't get unpleasant surprises from your decisions and think that you act fairly. But paying excessive homage to the principle of consistency can lead to inflexibility and being over-predictable.

There is not one type of leader who is equally successful in all circumstances. Winston Churchill was the right war-time leader because he had the natural qualities required by the situation, such as audacity, pugnaciousness and tenacity; but they did not serve him particularly well in peace-time. His successor, Clement Attlee, had none of the charisma of Churchill and would not have made an effective leader in war-time; but it is generally recognized that he was one of the best peace-time cabinet leaders in living memory.

Leaders emerge in certain situations because they have the qualities or the know-how needed – authority flows to the one who knows. In Barry's *The Admirable Crighton*, the butler became the leader when the family was shipwrecked on a desert island, because he was the man of the moment, the only one who could cope with the situation.

Factors influencing success

Successful leadership therefore seems to depend on having the right qualities at the right time. But what are the factors that influence and develop these qualities? A study of chief executives in the UK by Charles Margerison produced the following ranked list of influences on success:

		Rating out of 100
1.	Ability to work with people	78
2.	Early responsibility for important tasks	75
3.	A need to achieve results	75
4.	Leadership experiences early in career	74
5.	Wide experience in many functions before age of 35	68
6.	Ability to do deals and negotiate	66
7.	Willingness to take risks	63
8.	Ability to have more ideas than colleagues have	62
9.	Having talents 'stretched' by immediate bosses	60
10.	Ability to change managerial style to suit occasion	58

This list is a mix of abilities or skills (1, 3, 6, 7, 8 and 10) and the types of experience that have developed those abilities (2, 4, 5 and 9). It highlights the fact that natural abilities are only part of the picture; they are nurtured by experience and the situations in which potential and existing leaders have found themselves.

Lance Secretan in his book *Managerial Moxie* emphasized the last point when he said that leadership was largely an acquired skill. To start with, he wrote, a leader needs intelligence, a positive attitude and a combination of the qualities of courage, shrewdness and common sense (Moxie is a slang word for these qualities). Successful leaders, as they gain experience, build on these natural talents and develop the wide range of skills they need.

Personality traits of successful leaders

To develop Secretan's point, while it may not be possible to be definite about the abilities or skills that unequivocally characterize effective leaders in all situations, there is good evidence that there are certain basic personality traits which tend to characterize leaders in a wide variety of situations. In general, leaders are more intelligent than their followers, although not too much so, as they might appear to be remote and could have difficulties in communicating and getting their views accepted. Leaders also tend to be better adjusted, more dominant, more extrovert, less conservative, and to have a better understanding of people than the rank-and-file. It is interesting to note that these characteristics are sometimes latent and only emerge when people are put into leadership positions: 'Some are born great, some achieve greatness and some have greatness thrust upon them.'

Types of leader

Leaders can be defined in terms of characteristics, success factors and personality traits. To answer the question, 'Who is a leader?' it is also helpful to explore how these combine to produce different types of leader.

Leadership types can be classified in a number of ways and the following are some of the most typical categorizations:

1. *Charismatic/non-charismatic*: the charismatic leader relies on his aura, his personality and his inspirational qualities. These are natural characteristics, although experience may have taught him how best to project himself. The non-charismatic leader relies mainly on his know-how, his ability to give an impression of quiet confidence, and his cool analytical approach to dealing with problems.
2. *Autocratic/democratic*: the autocratic leader imposes his decisions and surrounds himself with yes-men. He uses his position to force people to do what they are told. The democratic leader encourages people to participate and involve themselves in decision taking. He will exert his authority to get things done but he will rely more on know-how and persuasive ability than the use of position power.
3. *The visionary/enabler or the controller/manipulator*: Dr John Nicholls identifies the visionary/enabler as the true leader, inspiring people with his vision of the future and using 'tender loving care' to encourage them to participate and to generate commitment. In contrast, the controller/manipulator is the administrator who is concerned essentially with operating the internal system and treating his subordinates with 'thinly disguised contempt'.

Of course, not one of the three contrasting types can be used as a description of a typical leader. Most leaders combine something of all these approaches in the way in which they carry out their task. The mix will depend on the make-up of the leader but also on the conditions under which he operates.

What followers expect from leaders

Followers want to feel that they are being led in the right direction. They want to be told where they are going and why. They need to know where they stand, what is going to happen and what is going to be in it for them. They want to feel that it is all worthwhile. That is why the visionary leader, who can somehow get across his inspiration to his team, usually gets the best results.

Research into the follower's perception of the leader, as summarized by Krech and Crutchfield, has indicated four requirements if the leader is to be successful.

1. *The leader must be perceived as 'one of us'*: he shares certain characteristics with the members of his group and is not perceived as an outsider.
2. *The leader must be perceived as 'most of us'*: he must incorporate to a special degree the norms and values which are central to the group. He can influence values by his visionary powers but he may fail as a leader if he moves too far away from them.
3. *The leader must be perceived as the 'best of us'*: he has to demonstrate that he is an expert in the task facing the group, indeed that he is superior to his team in those abilities which are relevant to the group task, ie getting the group working purposefully together. He need not necessarily have more expertise than each of his team members in particular aspects of the task, but he must prove that he can direct and harness this expertise in obtaining results.
4. *The leader must fit the followers' expectations*: he is more likely to gain the respect and co-operation of his followers if he behaves in a way which they expect of good leaders. These expectations will vary according to the group but will often include being straight, fair and firm as well as being considerate, friendly and approachable.

It is not enough, however, to define a leader in terms of who he is or what his followers think of him. He must also be considered from the point of view of what he does – his roles, the demands made upon him and the type of authority he exercises. These aspects of leadership are considered in the next section.

WHAT DO LEADERS DO?

Leadership is often described in military terms such as, 'Up boys and at 'em!' Business often uses military rhetoric: we all talk about tactics, strategy, campaigns etc. So before considering what leaders do, it is interesting to consider what they do not or should not do, as illustrated by the elements of military incompetence listed by Dixon:

1. A serious waste of human resources.
2. A fundamental conservatism and clinging to outworn tradition.
3. A tendency to reject or ignore information which is unpalatable or which conflicts with preconceptions.
4. A tendency to underestimate the enemy.
5. Indecisiveness and a tendency to abdicate from the role of decision maker.
6. An obstinate persistence in a given task despite strong contrary evidence.
7. Failure to exploit a situation gained and a tendency to 'pull punches'.
8. Failure to make adequate reconnaissance.
9. A predilection for frontal assaults, often against the enemy's strongest point.
10. A belief in brute force rather than the clever ruse.
11. Failure to make use of surprise or deception.
12. An undue readiness to find scapegoats.
13. A suppression of distribution of news from the front, usually deemed necessary for morale or security.
14. A belief in mystical forces – fate, bad luck etc.

You should not find it too difficult to find examples of all these mistakes being made by leaders you know or have heard of. There are many reasons for incompetence, among them being rigidity, lack of imagination and a dependence on outdated or ill-digested theories. The man who says he does not believe in theories and relies on practical experience can, paradoxically, be a dangerous theorist because he is deriving his ideas of what should be done (theories) from his own interpretation of his past experience, which could be selective, limited, superficial, prejudiced or outdated.

The biggest trap that leaders can fall into is being simplistic. Leadership is a complex process because it deals with complex situations and complex human beings; the leader has many different roles to play.

Leadership roles

Leadership roles can be classified into two groups:

1. *Primary functions,* which are essential to the process of leadership, namely:
   - *the leader as visionary*: he has a vision of the future and conveys his belief to his team;
   - *the leader as executive*: he determines the objectives of the group and directs and co-ordinates the group's activities in achieving them;
   - *the leader as planner*: he decides how the group should achieve its ends;
   - *the leader as policy maker*: he participates in formulating policies in the shape of continuing guidelines on what the group docs;
   - *the leader as expert*: he has the expertise and information required by the group;
   - *the leader as controller of relationships in the group*: he decides how the group should be organized and influences how people in the group work together;
   - *the leader as purveyor of rewards and punishments*: he has the power to apply rewards and punishments and thus exercise control over group members.
2. *Accessory functions,* which are those a leader may assume or be assigned because of his leadership position, namely:
   - *the leader as exemplar*: he serves as a model of behaviour for the group members;
   - *the leader as symbol of the group*: he provides a focus for group unity;
   - *the leader as father figure*: he can become an object for identification or even submissiveness;
   - *the leader as scapegoat*: he may become the target for the aggressions of a frustrated, disappointed, disillusioned group.

Demands made on the leader

The way in which a leader carries out these roles will be dependent on the two essential demands made on him. He has to:

1. *Achieve the task*: that is why he and his group exist. The leader's role is to ensure that the group's purpose is fulfilled. If it is not, the result is frustration, disharmony, criticism and eventually, perhaps, disintegration of the group.

2. *Maintain effective relationships*: between himself and the group and the people in it, and within the group. These relationships are effective if they are conducive to achieving the task. They can be divided into those concerned with the team and its morale and sense of common purpose, and those concerned with the individual and how he is motivated.

John Adair has suggested that these demands are best expressed as three areas of need which the leader is there to satisfy. These are:

1. *Task needs*: to get the job done.
2. *Group needs*: to build up and maintain team spirit.
3. *Individual needs*: to harmonize the needs of the individual with the needs of the task and the group.

These three needs are interdependent and are best expressed as the three overlapping circles shown in Figure 6.1. The leader's action in one area affects the others. Successful achievement of the task is essential if his team is to be held together or the individual is to be motivated to give his best effort to the job. Efforts directed at meeting group or individual needs stem directly from the needs of the leader to achieve the task. If any need is neglected, one of the others will suffer and the leader will be less successful.

Figure 6.1 *The three-circles model of leadership needs (John Adair)*

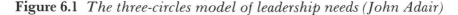

The authority of a leader

In taking action in each of these areas, but especially when satisfying task needs, the leader exercises authority, of which there are three types:

1. The authority of *position*: job title or rank.
2. The authority of *personality*: the ability to inspire, to persuade, to get people to 'follow my leader'.
3. The authority of *knowledge*: managerial, technical or professional.

Position authority may provide the starting point, but it can only be sustained and used effectively by deploying the second and third kinds of authority. This means using natural abilities and know-how in the light of an understanding of how leaders carry out their functions, with particular reference to their methods of dealing with task and people needs in accordance with the demands of the situation, as discussed in the next section.

HOW DO LEADERS DO IT?

Chester Barnard, chief executive of General Electric said that:

> A good leader may sometimes give the impression that he is a rather stupid fellow, an arbitrary functionary, a mere channel of communication, and a filcher of ideas. In a measure this is correct. He has to be stupid enough to listen a good deal, he certainly must arbitrate to maintain order and he has to be at times more a centre of communication. If he used only his own ideas he would be somewhat like a one-man orchestra, rather than a good conductor, who is, or should be, the very essence of a leader.

The analysis of what leaders do underlines the important point that the leader and his group are interdependent. He leads, they follow; but he depends just as much on them as they do on him. Eric Carlson's views, quoted in Chapter 2, are entirely relevant. He believes that the leader, while influencing his subordinates, has to treat them as respected and trusted. He shares Chester Barnard's view that employees in a sense delegate upwards to management the authority for organizational decisions and in so doing legitimize the right of those above to command those below.

The analysis does not, however, tell us exactly how it is done. Leadership still seems a somewhat abstract notion, and one of the dangers in trying to analyse leadership in these terms is that you end up being mystified by it; as the commanding officer of Robert Graves found in World War One, when he said that: 'Soldiers will follow this young officer if only to find out where he is going.'

A number of theories about leadership behaviour have been developed by academics. When you read the word theory – before reaching for your gun like Goering confronted with culture – remember that there is nothing so practical as a *good* theory, ie one based on proper observation, research and analysis, where actual results and the behaviours contributing to these results are studied by qualified people. Two of these research projects are described below. They expand on the distinction between task and people needs referred to above, and consider relationships between leadership behaviour and productivity. These researches contribute to a better understanding of how leaders function in different situations.

Two American researchers, Halpin and Winer, were asked to study leadership in aircrews in order to help in the selection of captains. The study was conducted by obtaining data on how existing commanders carried out their leadership functions, and what both their superiors and subordinates thought about them.

The research revealed two main dimensions of leadership which were described as:

1. *Initiating structure* (task-oriented): organizing and defining the task and the relationships between the captain and the crew.
2. *Consideration* (people-oriented): behaviour indicative of friendship, trust, respect and warmth in relationships between captain and crew. This is called the 'maintenance' function, ie the emphasis is on maintaining good relationships.

Typical actions under the heading of initiating structure included:

- He makes his attitude clear to his crew.
- He rules with an iron hand.
- He makes sure his role is understood by the crew.
- He maintains definite standards of performance.

Typical actions under the heading of consideration included:

- He finds time to listen to crew members.
- He looks out for the welfare of individual crew members.
- He treats crew members as his equals.
- He is friendly and co-operative.

One of the most interesting things about this study was that while superiors thought that the most effective captains were strongest in initiating structure, crew members thought that the best captains were equally strong on structure and consideration.

This distinction between being task- and people-oriented is not a black and white one. Most managers fall between these extremes and Blake and Mouton produced a grid, shown in Figure 6.2, against which managers are able to determine where they stand. According to their position on the grid, Blake and Mouton characterized management styles as:

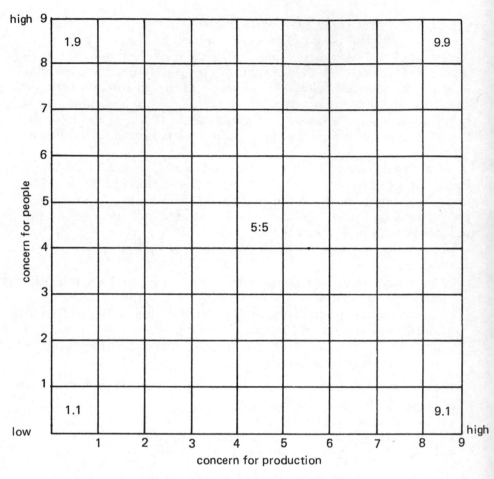

Figure 6.2 *The managerial grid*

- *9:1 style*: concentrates on the task, ignores the people. 'I get my job done in spite of my subordinates.'
- *1:9 style*: runs a cosy country club, looks after people and values friendly relations more than productivity. 'We have a cheerful crew but we haven't repaired many engines.'
- *1:1 style*: has little concern for people or production. 'My main aim is to keep my job and stay out of trouble.'
- *9:9 style*: obtains high productivity through gaining commitment. 'How can I harness group energy to achieve high productivity?'
- *5:5 style*: is the compromise man who produces as much as possible without upsetting people. 'Let's not be too demanding as long as we get a reasonable day's work done.'

Leadership and productivity

A number of studies in leadership and productivity have been carried out by Katz and Kahn among railway, engineering and insurance workers. They found that three dimensions of leadership behaviour were consistently related to productivity:

1. *Assumption of leadership role*: managers who actively assumed the functions of leadership were found to get better results than those who performed more or less the same functions as members of the group. The leader has to distance himself somewhat from the team. He cannot be one of the boys.
2. *Closeness of supervision*: high-production supervisors were found to supervise less closely than low-production supervisors. The latter tended, in various ways, to limit the freedom of the workers to do their jobs in their own way. Those who were allowed some autonomy on the job were more productive.
3. *Employee-orientation*: high-production supervisors were consistently found to be more employee-oriented and less production-oriented than low-production supervisors. But employee-orientation could be overdone. The best supervisors were interested in their staff in so far as they were effective producers; they did not coddle them nor did they set out to be liked. They maintained what Fielder terms 'psychological distance' between themselves and members of the group. They made it clear who was boss and discriminated sharply between competent and incompetent workers; encouraging and looking after the former and giving them considerable freedom to act, applying sanctions to the latter and restraining their autonomy.

The law of the situation

The type of leadership you exercise and your success as a leader depends to a large extent on the situation and your ability to understand it and act accordingly. The situation comprises the nature of the task, the impact of the organization (its policies, culture and environment), the degree to which the situation is structured or ambiguous, the sort of people you have in your working group, and the type of authority the leader has – given or assumed.

The performance of a group, as Fiedler pointed out, is related to both the leadership style and the degree to which the situation provides the leader with the opportunity to exert influence. His research indicated that a task-oriented/initiating structure approach works best for leaders and situations which are highly favourable. In the very favourable conditions when the leader has power, formal backing and a relatively well-structured task, the group is ready to be directed and told what to do.

In unfavourable conditions such as an emergency, the task-oriented leader will be more effective than the considerate leader who is concerned with interpersonal relationships. The latter will do better in a somewhat unstructured or ambiguous situation, or where his power as a leader is restricted.

Fiedler called this his 'contingency theory of leadership' and emphasized the situational aspects of being a leader:

> Leadership performance then depends as much on the organization as on the leader's own attributes. Except perhaps for the unusual case, it is simply not meaningful to speak of an effective leader or an ineffective leader, we can only speak of a leader who tends to be effective in one situation and ineffective in another.

The point was made earlier that not only does the situation affect the type of leadership required, but that it will also create conditions under which new and different types of leaders will emerge who are appropriately qualified to meet changing demands. Business leaders like Lee Iacocca of Chrysler, John Harvey-Jones of ICI and Michael Edwardes were put in positions where somehow they had to transform ailing organizations. In the *Transformational Leader,* Noel Tichy and Mary Devanno wrote of this sort of situation: 'Strategy's transformation of organizations is not something that occurs solely through the idiosyncratic behaviour of charismatic geniuses. It is a discipline with a set of predictable steps.' Transformational leaders, say Tichy and Devanno, have a fresh vision of the future and then take steps to communicate and institutionalize it. They do not wait for the danger to strike; instead they create a sense of urgency in the organization before an emergency occurs. If there is a threat, they sense it first and then transmit it to the rest of the organization so that all the people who matter can pre-empt it.

Leadership style

Following Fielder's analysis, the most effective leaders fit their style to the situation, which includes their own preferred style of operating and personal characteristics, as well as the nature of the task and the group.

Leadership style is the way in which you exercise your leadership role. It characterizes your approach to managing people. Leadership styles tend to be defined as extremes:

authoritarian	democratic
autocratic	participative
job-centred	people-centred
close, directive	general, permissive

In fact, good managers flex their styles between the extremes. There is no one style appropriate to all situations; you must be prepared to adjust your style according to the circumstances. This does not imply inconsistency. Effective leaders adopt the same approach in similar circumstances.

A continuum of leadership behaviour based on the work of Tannenbaum and Schmidt (Figure 6.3) suggests that there are five basic styles:

- *Tells*: the leader decides what to do and tells the individual to do it.
- *Sells*: the leader decides what to do but explains why it has to be done.
- *Tests*: the leader decides the lines along which he wants to act before committing himself, seeks opinions and, if necessary, modifies his decision.
- *Consults*: the leader defines the problem, proposes alternative courses of action and seeks suggestions on the action to be taken.
- *Joins*: the leader defines the problem and joins the process of working out alternative courses of action, evaluating them and making the final decision.

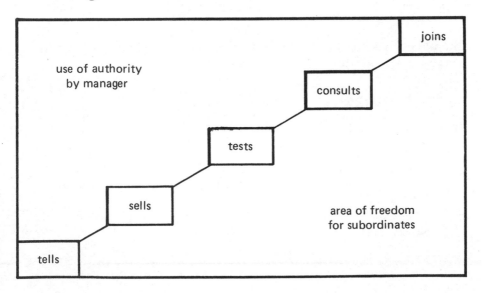

Figure 6.3 *Continuum of leadership behaviour*

These styles move from the authoritarian to the democratic, but it is not suggested that one is better than another. There will be circumstances when the manager has to tell someone to do something; at other times he may have to sell the idea or consult his subordinates in one way or another. Your job as a leader is to analyse the situation and apply the most appropriate style in accordance with your own knowledge of your capabilities and limitations.

These ideas were taken on board by Kenneth Blanchard who, in *Leadership and the One Minute Manager,* advocated situational leadership – 'different strokes for different folks' – and emphasized that there is no best leadership style. His four basic leadership styles are:

- *Directing*: giving specific instructions and supervising closely.
- *Coaching*: explaining directives, getting ideas and providing guidance.
- *Supporting*: sharing the process of decision making and providing support to subordinates in completing their tasks.
- *Delegating*: giving responsibility for decision making and problem solving to subordinates.

Blanchard also harked back to the other leadership dimensions when he distinguished between:

- *Directive behaviour*: defined by the words structure, control and supervise.
- *Supportive behaviour*: defined by the words praise, listen and facilitate.

But he emphasized that either kind of behaviour can be appropriate if the situation requires it.

LEADERSHIP SKILLS

If you want to be an effective leader you have to do six things:

1. Know yourself.
2. Know your situation.
3. Select leadership styles which are appropriate to the situation.
4. Satisfy task needs.
5. Satisfy team needs.
6. Satisfy individual needs.

Know yourself

As a leader, you will start with certain natural abilities and by experience you will develop certain skills. To improve your leadership qualities your first step is an analytical one – know yourself. Check each of the ten qualities and skills listed below and see how you measure up to them.

1. Ability to work with people.
2. Ability to gain the respect and support of people.
3. Decisiveness.
4. Enthusiasm.
5. Imagination (vision).
6. Ability to inspire others with your enthusiasm and vision.
7. Willingness to work hard.
8. Analytical ability.
9. Integrity.
10. Ability to change leadership style to suit occasion.

Assess your strengths and weaknesses under each heading. Analyse the occasions when you have succeeded *or failed*, and why. Try to assess how you exercised these abilities or skills and answer these questions:

- Was it directive?
- Was it supportive?
- Was it appropriate to the situation?
- Did it work? and if so why? and if not, why not?

If, following this analysis, you know your strengths, you can develop them and, if you know what works in particular circumstances, you will have a good idea of the approach you should adopt in similar situations (as long as they *are* similar). If you are aware of your weaknesses you can do your best to manage them, remembering, however, that there is no point in trying to invent an entirely new persona. As Robert Browning said: 'Best be yourself, imperial, plain and true.'

Know your situation

Having got to know something about yourself as a leader – your strengths and weaknesses – you have to carry on using your analytical powers to understand the situation so that you can exploit your strengths, minimize your weaknesses and adopt the most appropriate management style. Your situational analysis should answer the following questions:

1. *The task:*
   - what needs to be done, and why?
   - what results have to be achieved?

- what problems will have to be overcome?
- is the solution to these problems straightforward or is there a measure of ambiguity?
- is this a crisis situation?
- what is the timescale for completing the task?
- what pressures am I going to have exerted on me?

2. *The team:*
- what is the composition of the team?
- how well is the team organized?
- do the members of the team work well together?
- what will they want to get out of this?
- how am I going to get this particular team's commitment?
- how am I going to get results by satisfying their needs?
- how are they likely to respond to the various leadership styles or approaches I might adopt?

3. *The individuals in the team:*
- what are the strengths and weaknesses of each member of the team?
- what sort of things are likely to motivate them?
- how are they likely to respond individually to the various leadership techniques or styles I might adopt?

Select an appropriate leadership style

Adopt a situational approach to leadership by using your analyses of yourself, the task, the team and its individual members to decide on the most appropriate style or styles to adopt. The styles available to you are as shown in Figure 6.3: tell, sell, test, consult, join. Be prepared to flex your style in accordance with the changing needs of the task and the group and the variety of individual needs present among the members of your team.

Satisfy task needs

You will have been appointed to your task and given the authority and rank to do it, but you still have to earn the respect and enthusiasm of your group in order to complete the task successfully. You do this by demonstrating to your team that you:

1. Know where you are going: convey your vision of what you want to do and your enthusiasm for it. Define precisely the objectives of the assignment.

2. Know how you are going to get there: structure your team appropriately and make and communicate clear plans for achieving your objectives.
3. Know what you expect each member of your team to achieve, ensuring that work programmes, targets and standards of performance are clearly defined and understood by all concerned.
4. Know what you are doing: deal with problems decisively as they occur, progress the completion of the task in accordance with the programme, adapt the task as necessary, and provide the expertise and guidance the less experienced members of the team need.

Satisfy team needs

In satisfying task needs you will have provided the structure within which your team should be able to work well. To ensure that this happens you need to build up team spirit and morale. You have to induce in your team a feeling of shared responsibility for achieving results. You must establish and maintain mutual confidence and trust and create feelings of interdependence. You do this by:

1. Involving the group in agreeing objectives and reviewing results.
2. Ensuring that communications flow freely between all members of the team.
3. Encouraging informal meetings and contacts between members.
4. Taking steps to resolve unnecessary conflict but recognizing that differences of opinion, if sensibly discussed, can be productive.
5. Being approachable but maintaining sufficient distance from the group to be able to use your authority when the occasion demands it.

Satisfy individual needs

To satisfy individual needs you should ensure that each member of your team:

1. Feels a sense of personal achievement in the work he is doing.
2. Receives adequate recognition for his achievements.
3. Feels that the job is challenging, is demanding the best of him and is giving him the opportunity to use his abilities.
4. Knows that he is advancing in experience and knowledge, but also appreciates what he must do to improve his performance.

5. Understands what rewards he will get for good performance and what will happen if he fails. This means giving positive feedback for success, ie praise and rewards, and negative feedback for failure, ie constructive criticisms or disciplinary sanctions.

7. Getting the Message Across

WHY DOES IT MATTER?

Human resource management is as much about getting your message across as anything else. If the vision of the chief executive or any other manager is to get the deserved results, it is essential to communicate this vision in a way that will not only inform but also inspire those at the receiving end. They must understand the aims and values of the company and be persuaded to accept that the success of the company is in their own interests as well as those of the management.

John Garnett, the leading expert on communications, wrote:

> The success of managers depends, primarily, on their ability to communicate to all the people for whom they are responsible what they need to do and the importance of doing it. It involves the acceptance of change, the commitment to customer service, the achievement of more with less in the public service, and, the creation of the where without on which the future of the nation and the provision of jobs depends.

Failure to get the message across is costly. If you do not succeed, people will find it difficult to accept the need for improvement or change, they will not understand what is expected of them and they are unlikely to co-operate in drives to increase productivity. In short, they will not identify with the aims of the organization. To make this happen you must take the trouble to put on a show – all business is show business.

Getting it back

While getting it across is important you must not forget the value of getting it back, that is, obtaining views and ideas from further down in the organization. 'Communication is a two-way process, upwards as well as downwards', may be a cliché but it is none the less valid for that.

103

Wisdom is not uniquely located at the top. It is distributed throughout the organization and it must be shared and used everywhere.

WHAT DO YOU NEED TO KNOW AND DO?

One of the most familiar remarks in any organization is that, 'there's been a failure in communications around here'. There are four reasons for such failures:

1. People are unaware of the need to communicate.
2. People do not know what to communicate.
3. People do not know how to communicate.
4. Proper channels for communication are not available.

The first problem can be solved by continuous education and guidance. You have to communicate to people the need to communicate. To do this well, you must know how to deal with the other reasons for failure, and these are covered in the remaining sections of this chapter, as follows:

- What to communicate is considered from the point of view of what management wants to say and what employees want to hear. The various areas for communications are then discussed.
- How to communicate is considered first by dealing with the process of communication. The barriers to communication and methods of overcoming these barriers are then discussed.
- Facilities for communication are dealt with first by describing a key communications technique, team briefing, and then by reviewing other channels of communication such as newsletters and notice boards.

These approaches to communication all deal with getting the message across, although team briefing can be used to obtain feedback. The other methods of getting the message back – joint consultation and quality circles – are described in Chapter 15.

WHAT TO COMMUNICATE

You need to develop a strategy for communication and this should be based on analyses of what management wants to say and what employees want to hear.

What management wants to say

You should define three aims:

1. To get people to understand and accept what management proposes to do in areas that affect them.
2. To get people to act in the way management wants.
3. To get people to identify themselves more closely with the company and its achievements and to help them appreciate more clearly the contribution they make to these achievements.

Communications from management should be about plans, intentions and proposals (with the opportunity for feedback from employees) as well as about achievements and results. Exhortations should be kept to a minimum, if used at all; no one listens to them. You should concentrate on specific requirements rather than resorting to general appeals for such abstract things as improved quality or productivity. The requirements should be phrased in a way which emphasizes how all concerned will actually work together and the mutual benefits that should result.

What employees want to hear

Employees want to hear and comment upon the matters that affect their interests. These will include changes in working methods and conditions, company plans which may affect pay or security, and changes in terms and conditions of employment. It is your job to understand what people want to hear and plan your communications strategy accordingly. Understanding can be gained by making formal enquiries, by means of attitude surveys, by asking employee representatives, and by analysing genuine grievances to see if improved communications could overcome them.

John Garnett suggests that managers should regularly 'walk the ship' in the way that good captains do in order to keep in touch with their crew. In other words, you should regularly walk round your office or the shop floor, chatting to people informally. In this way you get to know them and they get to know you. The wrong sort of manager is someone who walls himself inside his own office and insists on his staff coming to see him, while never being seen in anyone else's office (except his boss's).

Areas for communication and the objective for each area are set out in Table 7.1.

Communication Area	Objectives
The communication downwards and sideways of corporate or functional objectives, policies, plans and budgets to those who have to implement them.	To ensure that managers and supervisors receive clear, accurate and prompt information on what they are expected to achieve to further the company's objectives.
The communication downwards of direct instructions from a manager to a subordinate on what the latter has to do.	To ensure that the instructions are clear, precise and provide the necessary motivation to get people into action.
The communication upwards and sideways of proposals, suggestions and comments on corporate or functional objectives, policies and budgets from those who have to implement them.	To ensure that managers and supervisors have adequate scope to influence corporate and functional decisions on matters about which they have specific expertise and knowledge.
The communication upwards and sideways of management information on performance and results.	To enable management to monitor and control performance so that, as necessary, opportunities can be exploited or swift corrective action taken.
The communication downwards of information on company plans, policies or performance.	To ensure that: 1) employees are kept informed of matters that affect them, especially changes to working conditions, and factors influencing their prosperity and security; 2) employees are encouraged to identify themselves more completely with the company.
The communication upwards of the comments and reactions of employees to what is proposed will happen or what is actually happening in matters that affect them.	To ensure that employees are given an opportunity to voice their suggestions and fears and that the company is in a position to amend its plans in the light of these comments.
The receipt and analysis of information from outside which affects the company's interests.	To ensure that the company is fully aware of all the information on legislation and on marketing, commercial, financial and technological matters that affects its interests.
The presentation of information about the company and its products to the government, customers and the public at large.	To exert influence in the interests of the company, to present a good image of the company and to persuade customers to buy its products or services.

Table 7.1

THE PROCESS OF COMMUNICATION

To get your message across more effectively you need to understand the process of communication. Otherwise you may fall into the same trap as Professor Spooner who, when asked why he was pumping the front tyre of his bicycle when it was the rear tyre that was flat, observed: 'And do they not communicate?'

Communication starts with the communicator wanting to say something; he then decides how it will be said and transmitted. The communication arrives with the recipient, who forms an impression of what he has heard and interprets it against his own background of attitudes and experiences. The process is illustrated in Figure 7.1.

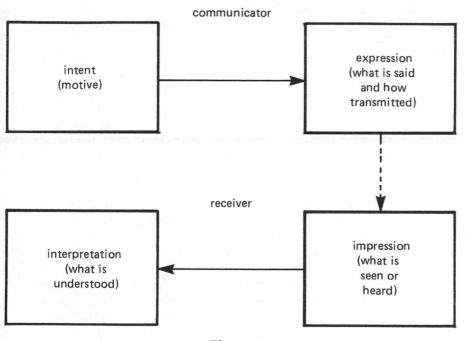

Figure 7.1

The basic problem in communications is that the meaning which is actually received by one person may not be what the other intended to send. The communicator and the receiver are two people living in different worlds; any number of things can happen to distort the messages that pass between them. People's needs and experiences tend to colour what they see and hear. Messages they do not want to hear are repressed, while others are magnified, created out of thin air or distorted from their original reality.

COMMUNICATION BARRIERS

So many barriers exist to good communications that the constant cry in all organizations that communications are bad is hardly to be wondered at – it is amazing that any undisturbed messages get through. Even if people try to communicate, they often fail. It is as Schopenhauer said: 'People are like hedgehogs, they want to communicate but their prickles keep them apart.'

The main barriers to communication are:

- *Ignoring information that conflicts with what we already know*: we tend to ignore or reject communications that conflict with our own beliefs. If they are not rejected, some way is found of twisting and shaping their meaning to fit our own preconceptions.
- *Perceptions about the communicator*: not only does the receiver evaluate what he hears in terms of his own background but he also takes the sender into account. Prejudice may ascribe non-existent motives to the communicator. Some people see every collective action as a subversive conspiracy.
- *Group influences*: the group with which we identify influences our attitudes and feelings. What a group 'hears' depends on its own interests. Shared experiences and common frames of reference will have more influence than exhortations from managers with whom employees feel they have nothing in common; and vice versa.
- *Words mean different things to different people*: words can have a special meaning to some people, with the result that they convey an impression different from the one intended. 'Profits' to management are an essential prerequisite to survival and growth. To the shop floor, they represent ill-gotten gains from exploiting the workers. Do not assume that something which has a certain meaning to you will convey the same meaning to someone else.
- *Jargon*: we all tend to use special language or 'jargon'. It is a convenient way of communicating between those in the know, but it is an effective and irritating barrier between those who know and those who do not.
- *Emotional context*: our emotions colour our ability to convey or to receive the true message. When we are insecure or worried, what we hear seems more threatening than when we are secure and at peace with the world.
- *Noise*: outside factors can interfere with the reception of the message. These may be literal noise which prevents words being heard, or figurative noise in the shape of distracting, confused or unclear information which distorts the message.

- *Size*: the sheer size and complexity of modern organizations can interfere with communications. Too many levels in an organization are one reason why messages get distorted.

Overcoming barriers

To overcome these barriers you need to:

1. *Adjust to the world of the receiver*: work out how he will perceive the message, understand his needs and potential reactions, use empathy, put yourself in his shoes.
2. *Use feedback*: get a message back from the receiver which tells you how far understanding has taken place.
3. *Use reinforcement*: present the message in a number of different ways to get it across. Use different channels of communication, the spoken as well as the written word.
4. *Use face-to-face communication*: this is more effective than the written word because you can observe the effect of what you say and get feedback from the receiver. You can then adjust your message.
5. *Use direct, simple language*: this seems all too obvious, but many people don't, and communication suffers accordingly.
6. *Reinforce words with actions*: if you say you are going to do something, do it. Your words become and remain credible.
7. *Reduce problems of size*: cut down the number of levels of management, reduce spans of control, ensure that activities are grouped on the basis of ease of intercommunication in matters that concern them, decentralize authority into smaller, self-contained although accountable units. For the purposes of good communications 'small is beautiful'. It is the contact that counts.

CHANNELS OF COMMUNICATION

The nine main channels of communication available to help you get it across are:

1. Person-to-person contact.
2. Team briefing.
3. Video.
4. Magazines.
5. Newsletters.
6. Bulletins.
7. Notice boards.
8. Consultative committees.
9. Quality circles.

Person-to-person

This is the best communication channel of all. You get direct and immediate feedback and you are in the ideal position to 'adjust to the world of the receiver'. You can modify your approach and place different emphases on your messages in accordance with the reaction of your listener. This means meeting people on their home ground, in their offices, on the shop floor. It involves MBWA – management by walking about – so that you can see and be seen, speak and be spoken to. Leadership is about impressing your personality on other people. What better way to do it than through person-to-person contact rather than through video tape or even print?

Team briefing

Person-to-person contact may be the ideal, but the chief executive cannot be everywhere at once. He must often rely on other people to get his message across. The best way of doing this is by team briefing. This is a method of communication developed by the Industrial Society, which defines it as:

> A system of communication operated by line management. Its objective is to ensure that *all* employees know and understand what they and others in the company are doing and why. It is a management information system. It is based on the leader and his/her team getting together in a group for half an hour on a regular basis to talk about things that are relevant to their work.

Team briefing operates on the cascade system, ie communications or briefs start from the top and go steadily down, team by team, through the organization. However, team briefing can additionally take place within departments on matters that only affect their members. The main features of the process are:

1. *Organization:*
   - cover all levels in an organization;
   - fewest possible steps between the top and bottom;
   - between four and 18 in each group;
   - run by the immediate leader of each group at each level (who must be properly trained and briefed in his task).
2. *Subjects:*
   - policies – explanations of new or changed policies;
   - plans – as they affect the organization as a whole and the immediate group;

- progress – how the organization and the group are getting on, what the latter needs to do to improve;
- people – new appointments, points about personnel matters (pay, security, procedures).
3. *Timing and duration:*
   - ideally, a minimum of once a month for those in charge of others and once every two months for every individual in the organization – but meetings only take place if there is something to say;
   - duration not longer than 20-30 minutes.

The merit of team briefing is that it enables face-to-face communications to be planned and, to a reasonable degree, formalized. It is easy, however, for it to start in a wave of enthusiasm and then to wither away because of lack of sufficient drive and enthusiasm from the top downward, inadequately trained and motivated managers and supervisors, reluctance of management to allow subjects of real importance to be discussed throughout the system and insufficient feedback upwards through each level. A team briefing system must be led and controlled effectively from the top, but it does require a senior manager with specific responsibility to advise on the subject matter and the preparation of briefs (it is important to have well-prepared material to ensure that briefing is carried out consistently and thoroughly at each level), to train managers and supervisors, and to monitor the system by checking on the effectiveness and frequency of meetings.

Video

If you cannot see everyone and do not wish to rely on other people but still wish to be seen and heard, video may be the answer. Because it is a visual and live medium it can make much more impact than the printed word. It can get personal messages across and, if prepared properly, can present fairly complicated information about, for example, company activities and results, in a clear and entertaining way.

Magazines

Glossy magazines or house journals are an obvious way to keep employees informed about the company and they are often used for public relations purposes as well. They can extol and explain the achievements of the company and may thus help to increase identification and even loyalty. If employees are encouraged to contribute (although this is difficult), the magazine can become more human. The biggest danger of this sort of magazine is that it becomes a public relations type of exercise, which is seen by employees as having little relevance to their everyday affairs.

Newsletters

Newsletters aim to appear more frequently and to angle their contents more towards the immediate concerns of employees than the glossier forms of house magazine do. To be effective, they should include articles specifically aimed at explaining what management is planning to do and how this affects the company. To capture the attention of readers they can also include more chatty 'human interest' material about the doings of employees. Correspondence columns can provide an avenue for the expression of employees' views and replies from management, but no attempt should be made to censor letters (except those that are purely abusive) or to pull punches in reply. Anonymous letters should be published if the writer gives his name to the editor.

The key factor in the success of a newsletter or any form of house magazine is the editor. He should be someone who knows the company and its employees and can be trusted by everyone to be frank and fair. Professional expertise is obviously desirable but it is not the first consideration, as long as the individual can write reasonably well and has access to expert help in putting the paper together.

Companies often publish a newsletter in addition to a house magazine, treating the latter mainly as a public relations exercise and relying on the newsletter as the prime means of communicating with employees.

Bulletins

Bulletins can be used to give immediate information, which cannot wait for the next issue of a newsletter, to employees; or they can be a substitute for a formal publication if the company does not feel that the expense is justified. Bulletins are only useful if they can be distributed quickly and are seen by all interested employees. They can simply be posted on notice boards or, more effectively, given to individual employees and used as a starting point for a briefing session, if they contain information of sufficient interest to merit a face-to-face discussion.

Notice boards

Notice boards are an obvious but frequently misused medium for communications. The biggest danger is allowing boards to be cluttered up with uninteresting or out-of-date material. It is essential to control what goes on to the boards and to appoint responsible people to service them by removing out-of-date or unauthorized notices.

A more impressive show can be made of notices and other material if an information centre is set up in the canteen or some other suitable place, where the information can be displayed in a more attractive and compelling manner than on a typical notice board.

Consultative committees

Joint consultative committees exist to provide a channel for two-way communication. Sometimes, however, they are not particularly effective, either because their thunder has been stolen by union negotiating committees or because their proceedings are over-formalized and restricted. It is essential to disseminate the information revealed at committees around the offices and works, but it is impossible to rely on committee members to do this. Minutes can be posted on notice boards, but they are seldom read, usually because they contain too much redundant material.

Twelve rules for internal communications

To sum up, the following are the twelve golden rules for internal communications which were given by William Mercer, MPA at a recent conference:

1. There is no such thing as a stone cold certainty in business decision making, and it is important that everyone in a business realises this.
2. If a board cannot or will not spell out its business strategy clearly employees are entitled to assume it does not have one.
3. Assume that in an information vacuum people will believe the worst.
4. Never take it for granted that people know what you are talking about.
5. Always take it for granted that people doing a job know more about it than you do.
6. Telling people something once is not much better than not telling them at all.
7. Never assume that people will tell you anything that reflects unfavourably upon themselves.
8. Remember that employees read newspapers, magazines and books, listen to the radio and watch television.
9. Do not be afraid to admit you were wrong; it gives people confidence that you know what you are doing.

10. Asking for help, taking advice, consulting and listening to others are signs of great strength.
11. Communicating good news is easy but even this is often not done by management; bad news is often left to rumours and the grapevine.
12. Changing attitudes to change behaviour takes years: changing behaviour changes attitudes in weeks.

PART II

Human Resource Planning

Introduction

Human resource planning (HRP) ensures that the organization knows and gets what it wants in the way of the people needed to run the business now and in the future. It starts from the strategic objectives of the company and an analysis of the human resources required to achieve them. HRP sets out requirements in both quantitative (how many people) and qualitative (what sort of people) terms. It provides the basis for recruitment programmes (Chapter 9) as one of the main human resource systems, and for human resource development plans (Chapter 13).

8. Defining Requirements

The definition of requirements is based on a human resource information system which provides the basis for human resource plans (longer term) and human resource budgeting (shorter term).

THE HUMAN RESOURCE INFORMATION SYSTEM

The management information system is used to prepare human resource statistics and analyse staff turnover or wastage so that demand and supply forecasts can be made and comparisons carried out between budgeted and actual figures. The first step is to establish the database.

Database

The database can be developed from personnel records and the payroll system. The major items for individual employees are:

1. *Personal data*: name, address, date of birth, marital status, next of kin, children, qualifications and special skills, training received.
2. *Position data*: current job and occupational history, work location, starting dates with company and for each job held in the company.
3. *Financial data*: current pay, pay history, merit, incremental, bonus, commission, shift and overtime payments, tax code, national insurance data, deductions from pay (eg voluntary savings), pension details, details of bank.

A computer-based system is desirable, even in smaller companies, and the development and use of such systems is discussed at the end of this section.

Analysis

The analysis of individual data can provide the following information to assist in human resource planning and budgeting:

- Headcounts of employees analysed by occupation, location, department, age, service, skills or grades.
- Numbers joining or leaving the company (the losses may be analysed by reasons for leaving).
- Wastage (staff turnover) rates, discussed in more detail below.
- Sickness and absenteeism rates.
- Comparisons of actual numbers employed with budgets.
- The salary and wages bill, actual and compared with budget.
- The amount of overtime (hours and cost), actual compared with budget.

Staff turnover

Staff turnover or labour wastage, as it is often called, is a measure of the number of leavers over a period of time. The traditional formula is the labour turnover index:

$$\frac{\text{number of leavers in a specified period (usually 1 year)}}{\text{average number of employees during the same period}} \times 100$$

If the average number of employees over a year is 200 and 30 of them leave during that year, the labour turnover index is:

$$\frac{30}{200} \times 100 = 15\%$$

Wastage figures should be analysed in order to forecast future losses and, therefore, requirements. The trends in wastage should be monitored to indicate any changes for better or worse in the rate at which employees leave the company. The reasons for leaving, which should be obtained at exit interviews, and recorded, are analysed to indicate where any action can be taken to reduce wastage.

Although high wastage levels are obviously worrying because of disruption and the cost of recruitment and training, too low a figure may suggest stagnation or even complacency. There are no firm guidelines on what levels of wastage are good or bad. It all depends on the circumstances, especially the type of people employed. As a very broad rule indeed, wastage of between 10 and 15 per cent a year in a work force which is fairly well balanced with regard to skills and the proportions of men and women, is often regarded as normal. The most important thing for you to keep an eye on is the trend in wastage, not the absolute level.

It may be simple, but the traditional formula can be misleading when the turnover rate is inflated by the high rate of wastage applying to a small proportion of the labour force. Thus, a company employing 500 people might have had a wastage rate of 15 per cent, meaning that 75 people had left during the year. This may have been spread throughout the company, covering all occupations, but it may have been restricted to a small sector of the labour force. For instance, 50 out of the 75 losses may have been accounted for by only five jobs, each of which had to be filled 10 times. Clearly the wastage problem in these circumstances would be quite different from a situation where turnover was spread over all or most of the 75 jobs.

To avoid this difficulty, it is necessary to look behind the raw percentages and check on the incidence of turnover in particular areas or occupations. You can also use the survival rate formula to provide additional data on losses. This measures the proportion of an intake of staff who are still with the company after a period of time. For example, if a firm recruits 20 graduates and after a year, 15 are still employed, the survival rate is 75 per cent. Survival rates can be used to compare the wastage levels between different occupations and also to forecast the number of replacements that will be required over a period of time.

Use of computers

Computers will hold human resource data in a compact and accessible way, and they can be justified for that reason alone. They can generate information for decision making in human resource planning and many other human resource system areas more flexibly, more quickly and more comprehensively than any manual system.

Selecting the computer system

The extent to which an organization will want to use any of the facilities provided by a computer, apart from the basic record keeping and listing functions, will vary according to its size, complexity and the importance it attaches to basing decisions on accurate and quickly provided information. Before selecting the system a cost/benefit analysis is required. Some savings in staff time and in space for storing records will be obvious; others will be more subjective. It is best to start in a fairly small way and add extra facilities as experience is gained. This implies, however, that the basic system must be flexible and able to be extended.

A flexible and not too ambitious approach is desirable. Control of the project should be vested in the personnel department – the user should always head the study, although he will have to accept technical advice on systems, feasibility and costs. Advice from internal systems analysts or, if they are not available, external consultants is obviously essential. The development should be staged, starting with a fairly modest record-keeping facility and extending to the more sophisticated applications as experience is gained. It is unwise to try to do too much too quickly. In designing the system, ease of operation, clarity of presentation, economy in use and flexibility are all important considerations.

Clearly, the choice of system will be strongly influenced by the uses to which it will be put. For example, if the system will need to answer questions rapidly, it is desirable to have an online (ie immediate access) facility to the data held in it. If it is to be used in modelling and posing 'what if?' questions, then the system will require sizeable computing power, particularly if large amounts of data are involved. This may rule out microcomputers and make it necessary to use a mainframe or at least a minicomputer.

A decision will have to be made on whether the personnel and payroll systems should be integrated. Much common data is held on these two systems and it would seem to make sense to combine them. Many companies operate a 'payroll-driven' system in which the basic payroll data is augmented by personnel information. Such systems are usually cheaper to introduce and operate than completely separate ones.

Finance departments often want to keep control over pay transactions and there is a danger of losing flexibility if the systems are too closely linked. A strong case can be made for a separate system doing what the personnel department wants it to do, but such systems can be costly to develop and use.

The choice of basic system lies between:

1. *A bureau*: this uses its own software (ie programs) on its own hardware (ie computer and peripheral equipment). Bureaux are used because they have the software and computer resources available and therefore relieve the client company of pressure on its own system development and hardware resources. It is usually cheaper to develop a system at a bureau than in-house, but a standard package has to be accepted which may not fit the company's needs.

2. *Internally developed software run on in-house hardware*: given the time, money and resources needed, this approach should provide the most appropriate and flexible system. The initial choice lies between using an existing mainframe or minicomputer or instal-ling a microcomputer for the personnel department's exclusive use. The latter alternative has some attractions on the grounds of accessibility and control but restricts the amount of data and

facilities available. There is, however, considerable cost and always some risk in developing new software, which is why alternative 3 below is sometimes adopted. There is also the risk that an internal mainframe or even a minicomputer might become overloaded, making access difficult. It is possible to avoid this problem by installing a microcomputer within the personnel department.

3. *Externally developed software run on in-house hardware*: this alternative reduces the cost and risk of developing special programs, but the result may not be so relevant to the company's needs.

Operating the computer system

The system needs to provide for the following operational requirements:

1. *Updating*: in a paper-driven system changes are originated on forms and either transcribed ready for punching or used to 'key in' the information directly (ie 'online'). Changes are often processed in batches. With most mini- or micro-based systems the updating is carried out not only online but also in 'real time'. This means that changes are immediately made to the record being updated rather than being processed some time later.

2. *Enquiries*: the ideal method is to have an online system, which means that enquiries can be answered immediately, using a terminal.

3. *Reports*: reports will be produced either on a routine or an *ad hoc* basis, depending on requirements and the programs available.

4. *Security*: a system has to be introduced to protect information and to prevent unauthorized changes being made to salaries, pay grades or other personal data. Access to the computer must be restricted to authorized individuals who will have to use 'blind' (ie secret) passwords before updating records or asking for information. Different levels of authority will have to be allocated.

Uses of the computer

In human resource planning, the computer system can generate forecasts of the future demand for and supply of people. The Institute of Manpower Studies has developed various models for this purpose. It is also possible to produce staff turnover statistics, such as wastage or survival rates, for the company as a whole or by occupation or department.

The other uses to which a computerized database can be put are:

1. *Keeping records*: replacing card indexes and filing cabinets by magnetic discs.
2. *Listings*: quickly providing listings of employees by department, occupation, grade, pay level, length of service, age, sex, qualifications, skills etc.
3. *Automatic letter writing*: producing standard letters and forms for recruitment, promotion, transfer, upgrading, appraisal, pay review and new contracts of employment.
4. *Career development*: as a development of manpower planning models, computerized personnel information can be used to improve succession planning.
5. *Recruitment*: the computer can, in effect, be used as a filing cabinet to store details of each applicant, date of receipt of application, when called for interview and the outcome. If an applicant contacts the company, he can rapidly be told the progress of his application. Managers can be given details of the number of applicants and how many have been interviewed. Lists and automatic letters can be produced when calling for interview, rejecting applicants or making offers.
6. *Training*: records can be kept to check on who has received training or on progress through apprenticeship or other training schemes. Listings of skills and qualifications by department or occupation can be produced to identify gaps and training needs.
7. *Pay*: information can be drawn from both personnel and payroll systems to analyse payroll costs and ratios and to assess the impact of various pay increase options on the pay structure and on total payroll costs. Budgetary control systems can be computerized to show actual payroll costs against budget and to project future costs.
8. *Salary administration*: salary analysis reports can be produced which give information by employee on occupation, salary, position in salary range, total and percentage increases over previous years and appraisal codes. Individual forms and departmental schedules can be generated for salary reviews and analyses can be made of the salary structure, actual and percentage increases in payroll costs against budget, distribution of staff in salary ranges and salary attrition (ie the extent to which the cost of merit increases is eroded over the year because of the movements of leavers and joiners into the salary system).
9. *Job evaluation*: databases can be created to hold and process information on job evaluation, such as grades and points scores. Weightings or job evaluation factors can be determined by multiple regression analysis, and the recording and analysis of

paired comparisons can be computerized. In a job evaluation exercise, the information system can be used to print out the names of those whose jobs are to be evaluated. Details of job, grade, function, location, sample size and current point ratings can be programmed in. The database can link together similar posts in different parts of the organization. Listings of all gradings, re-gradings and points scores can be produced.

10. *Absence and sickness*: absences can be recorded by employee, with reasons, and analyses produced of absenteeism and sickness. In the UK, the introduction of the Statutory Sickness Pay (SSP) scheme with all the recording which it entails has accelerated the use of computers as a database for sickness records.

11. *Health and safety*: records can be maintained on accidents and absence due to health hazards. Trends can be analysed and information produced on who has worked in certain areas, or who has used certain processes and for how long.

HRP AIMS

The aims of HRP are to ensure that the organization:

1. Obtains and retains the quantity and quality of human resources it requires.
2. Is able to anticipate the problems arising from potential surpluses or deficits of people.

HRP ACTIVITIES

The four HRP activities are:

1. *Demand forecasting*: estimating future human resource needs by reference to strategic business plans and forecasts of future levels of activity. These needs are expressed in terms both of the number of people required and of the skills and expertise needed. Any shift in the mix of skills or the requirement for new types of expertise arising from technological or other changes incorporated in the strategic plan should be assessed, so that plans can be made to recruit, train, re-train and develop the human resources the organization will need.
2. *Supply forecasting*: estimating the supply of people from inside and outside the organization by analysis.
3. *Determining human resource requirements*: analysing the demand and supply forecasts to identify future needs or surpluses.

4. *Action planning*: preparing and implementing plans to satisfy future human resource needs or to deal with surpluses.

Demand forecasting

There are four ways in which you can forecast demands for human resources:

1. *Managerial judgement*: this is the most typical method. It simply means that you sit down, think about future developments and workloads and then decide how many and what sort of people you need. The judgement may be based on rules of thumb about the relationship between activity levels and the requirement for people, plus a broad assessment of the impact of technological and other developments on human resource requirements. Essentially, however, it is guess work.

   In the short term, and if it is easy to get hold of people quickly, this method will get you by, but it is not a valid approach to longer-term planning or in conditions where there may be serious problems in getting or losing people.

2. *Ratio-trend analysis*: this is a more systematic approach to assessing the numbers required than managerial guess work. It is carried out by studying existing ratios between activity levels and the number of staff, or between the numbers of one type of employee compared with another, and then forecasting future needs by reference to changes in prime activity levels or staff numbers.

   For example, an activity-related forecast in an insurance company will be based on the existing ratio between the number of proposals dealt with in a week and the number of underwriters, which is, say, 1:300. A drive to expand business is expected to increase the total number of proposals received a week by, say, 1800. An extra six underwriters would therefore be required. This assumes that there will be no improvements in productivity arising from the use of new technology or better working methods. Allowances would have to be made for such changes, or indeed for any factor which might increase the complexity of the work and therefore reduce the quantities that would be handled by one person. Wherever possible the ratio between activity levels and numbers required should be determined by work study (see below).

   An example of a ratio-trend forecast based on the relationships between different categories of worker is in a manufacturing plant employing direct production workers and indirect workers such as inspectors. If the existing ratio of direct workers to inspectors is

10:1, a change in activity levels leading to a related change in the number of direct workers (established by ratio-trend analysis), indicates how many extra or fewer inspectors are required. The calculation is carried out like this:

- rate of activity levels to direct worker – 50 units:1
- forecast increase in activity levels – 1000
- extra direct workers required = 20
- ratio of direct workers to inspectors – 10:1 therefore extra inspectors required = 2.

3. *Work study*: the most accurate way to prepare numerical demand forecasts is to base them on work study. This requires the use of work measurement techniques which indicate how much time an operation or group of operations should take to complete and, therefore, the number of workers required, having made allowances for rest breaks, fatigue, absence and idle time. Work standards can then be produced, and the numbers needed are calculated by applying the standards to forecast volumes of work.

In a manufacturing department the starting point is the production budget, worked out from the planned manufacturing programme in which projected outputs are expressed in volume terms. The standard hours per unit of output as determined by work measurement are multiplied by the planned volume of units to be produced, to give the total planned hours for the period. This is divided by the number of actual working hours for an individual operator, to show the number of operators required. Allowance has to be made for absenteeism and forecast levels of idle time. A highly simplified example of this procedure is shown below.

Planned output for year	= 20,000 units
Standard hours per unit	= 5 hours
Planned hours for year	= 100,000 hours
Productive hours per man year (allowing for normal overtime, absenteeism and idle time)	= 1750
Number of direct workers required	= 57

In clerical functions where work measurement has been applied, it is possible to adopt the same approach of relating activity levels to standard hours and deriving a planned hour figure for conversion to the staff numbers required.

In areas where work measurement is difficult or impossible, such as technical departments and indirect functions like inspection, reliable work standards are difficult if not impossible to produce. Some companies have tried to develop notional standards for these activities, but they have usually proved to be unreliable. The best approach for these functions is to use ratio-trend forecasting which is related to the numbers of direct workers calculated by work measurement standards. Although somewhat crude, an approach that simply assesses the output that can reasonably be expected from a person over a period of time, eg 50 customer queries processed in a day, can provide a basis for relating future needs to forecast activity levels, which will always be better than guess work.

4. *Mathematical models*: to build a mathematical model for human resource planning you need to analyse past statistical data and to describe the relationships between a number of variables in a mathematical formula. The variables affecting human resource requirements may be identified under headings such as activity levels, investment, rates of production, or sales. The formula can then be applied to forecasts of movements in the parameters to produce a forecast. The effect of alternative assumptions on requirements can also be assessed.

   Mathematical models require a computer and can be expensive to create. Software HRP packages are, however, available, such as those developed by the Manpower Society.

5. *Skills/expertise analysis*: it is necessary to make a careful assessment of future changes in the current mix or range of skills and expertise which will arise from the strategic plans of the company, in so far as projected product and market developments and the introduction of new technology affect the sort of people needed. Although this may often be largely a matter of judgement, it is still essential to review every aspect of the corporate plan to assess its implications on the use of human resources.

Supply forecasting

Supply forecasting measures the quantity of human resource that is likely to be available from within the organization. Forecasts are based on:

1. *An analysis of existing resources* by occupation, level of skill, status and length of service. Movements in ratios between, for example, direct and indirect staff would be studied to provide guidance on trends and to indicate where future changes might result in supply problems.

2. *An analysis of wastage*: the rates at which different categories of employees are leaving, to produce forecasts of future replacement

requirements. The incidence of wastage in different areas and occupations and the reasons for leaving should also be examined as a guide to any action required to reduce losses.

3. *An assessment of changes in conditions of work and absenteeism*: the hours available in the future will obviously be affected by changes in standard hours of work, overtime policies, the length and timing of holidays, shift systems, retirement policy, and the policy for employing part-timers. The scope for work sharing should also be considered, that is, one job being split between two or possibly even more people, on the basis of one person doing the work for part of the day and another person or persons taking over the job for the rest of the day.

4. *Forecasting the output of training schemes*: these would include apprentices and other full-time training courses. The output forecast would take account of natural wastage during the training period, bearing in mind that wastage often increases quite considerably at the end of an apprenticeship, unless steps are taken to encourage ex-apprentices to stay.

Determining human resource requirements

Your future requirements are determined simply by bringing together the demand and supply forecasts. In the long term, say over two years, the manpower plans might be expressed in the form of targets to be achieved by the end of the year or at points during the year. In the shorter term, however, the plans would be broken down into the actual numbers to be recruited or released each week or month.

A 12-month target would be established by subtracting from existing numbers losses through wastage and adding the net output from training schemes to obtain the forecast number of people who will be available. This figure would be adjusted to allow for changes in hours or holidays and compared with the demand forecast to show how many extra or fewer people will be required. For example:

1. Current number of skilled fitters	120
2. Less wastage over year	–15
3. Plus net output over year from apprenticeship scheme	+5
4. Number available in 12 months' time (no changes in hours or holidays)	110
5. Number required in 12 months' time	130
6. Number to be recruited over the year	20

The recruitment programme could then be drawn up by reference to the dates when extra fitters are required, the likely incidence of losses and the dates when apprentices will become available.

Action planning

Action planning decides how human resource targets should be achieved and what needs to be done to deal with problems of major technological change, redundancy or high wastage. The main elements, depending on circumstances, are:

1. *The recruitment plan*, which will set out:
   - the numbers and types of people required and when they are needed;
   - any special supply problems and how they are to be dealt with;
   - the recruitment programme.
2. *The human resource development plan*, which will show:
   - the number of trainees or apprentices required and the programme for recruiting or training them;
   - the number of existing staff who need training or retraining and the training programme;
   - the new courses to be developed or the changes to be made to existing courses.
3. *The retention plan*, which will describe the actions required to reduce avoidable wastage under the following headings:
   - pay problems: increasing pay levels to meet competition; improving pay structures to remove inequities, altering payment systems to reduce extensive fluctuations; introducing procedures for relating rewards more explicitly to effort or performance;
   - employees leaving to further their career: providing better career opportunities and ensuring that employees are aware of them; extending opportunities for training; adopting and implementing 'promotion from within' policies and introducing more systematic and equitable promotion procedures; deliberately selecting employees who are not likely to want to move much higher than their initial job;
   - employees leaving because of conflict: introducing more effective procedures for consultation, participation and handling grievances; improving communications by such means as team briefing using the conflict resolution and team-building techniques of organization development programmes; reorganizing work and the arrangement of offices or workshops to increase group cohesiveness; educating and training manage-

ment in approaches to improving their relationships with employees;

- the induction crisis: improving recruitment and selection procedures to ensure that job requirements are specified accurately and that the people who are selected fit the specification; ensuring that candidates are given a realistic picture of the job, pay and working conditions; developing better induction and initial training programmes;
- shortage of labour: improving recruitment, selection and training for the people required; introducing better methods of planning and scheduling work to smooth out peak loads;
- changes in working requirements: ensuring that selection and promotion procedures match the capacities of individuals to the demands of the work they have to do; providing adequate training or adjustment periods when working conditions change; adapting payment by result systems to ensure that individuals are not unduly penalized when they are only engaged on short runs;
- losses of unstable recruits: taking more care to avoid recruiting unstable individuals by analysing the characteristics of applicants which are likely to cause instability and using this analysis to screen results.

4. *The redevelopment plan*, which will set out programmes for transferring or retraining existing employees.
5. *The redundancy plan*, which will indicate:
   - the extent to which surpluses of people can be absorbed by natural wastage, obviously the most desirable method;
   - who is to be redundant, where and when;
   - the scope for encouraging voluntary redundancy and the inducements that need to be offered;
   - the plans for redevelopment or retraining, where this has not been covered in the redevelopment plan;
   - the steps to be taken to help redundant employees find new jobs;
   - the policy for declaring redundancies and making redundancy payments;
   - the programme for consulting with unions or staff associations and informing those affected.

HUMAN RESOURCE BUDGETING

Your manpower plans should provide the basis for ensuring you get what you want in the way of people and are able to anticipate rather than just react to surplus or deficit problems. But your concern for human resources should extend beyond simply getting and keeping staff, to the need to control their use so as to increase productivity and avoid overmanning or waste.

Human resource utilization is dealt with in detail in Chapter 16. The starting point for getting the most out of people, however, is the human resource budget. This can be defined as a statement in quantitative and financial terms of the planned allocation and use of human resources to achieve a planned level of activity or volume of output.

Basic human resource budgeting

The basic budget is a quantitative statement of the number of employees required relative to budgeted output and activity levels. This quantitative statement is turned into a cost budget, which is a product of the number of people employed and their pay during the budget year.

The methods used to prepare the budget are similar to those used to produce human resource plans, ie managerial judgement, ratio-trend analysis, work study (the best approach, where feasible) or mathematical modelling. The approaches used for different categories of staff are dealt with below.

Direct production labour requirements

Where a detailed sales estimate or production programme exists, the amount of direct labour will depend on the budgeted output of the products in each cost centre, translated from physical units into planned hours by the application of standard hour per unit figures, if available. If standard hours cannot be used, a more subjective and less desirable method relying upon past experience and judgement will have to be adopted. The forecast should take account of anticipated performance levels where an incentive scheme is in operation, and allowance should be made for absenteeism and sickness.

When a detailed sales estimate or production programme is not available, for example, where jobbing work is undertaken, the estimate of direct labour requirements can be made by:

1. Relating the sales turnover of a previous period to the corresponding number of direct labour hours in each cost centre, and applying this ratio to the budgeted sales turnover for this period. Adjustments would have to be made for inflation and changes in selling prices.
2. Flexing the budget established by the above method to adjust standard hours and manning requirements to actual output levels.

Machine or process hour requirements

Where your pace of production is set by machines or processes, you will need first to calculate the machine or process hours applicable to the budgeted production load. If extra production can be taken up by spare machine or production line capacity, current manning standards will indicate how many extra workers will be needed. You should, however, subject these standards to careful scrutiny to see if they can be tightened up, always subject to persuading any trade union concerned to accept the change, which is unlikely to be easy.

If extra capacity is needed, the alternative ways of meeting the production targets should evaluated, eg overtime, extra shifts, night-work, subcontracting. The costs of these alternatives should be assessed against the cost of investing in new plant or a new production line, and the return that investment will achieve.

Indirect production labour

Indirect production labour, which is usually included in the direct expense budget of a production department, may tend to vary with the total production of a department rather than with the output of particular cost centres within it.

Indirect labour is difficult to measure and work standards are not usually available. The duties of indirect workers are furthermore often unpredictable or irregular. As a result, it has frequently been the custom to allot a certain number of such workers to a department, leaving it to the departmental manager and his supervisor to see that they are fully occupied. This is clearly undesirable.

You can, if you wish, use data on the ratio of indirects to directs as a starting point when assessing requirements, but existing ratios should not be taken at their face value. Managers should be required to justify the number of indirect workers they need on the basis of the work it is essential for them to do, rather than by reference to an historical ratio, which may simply perpetuate overmanning.

Clerical staff

Overmanning in clerical departments is rife. Management consultants who specialize in clerical work measurement can almost guarantee that they can cut staff numbers by 15 per cent or more without affecting output or quality. The reasons for this are fairly obvious and include:

- Lack of standards upon which to base human resource forecasts.
- Manning to meet peak loads rather than taking action either to smooth out peaks or to cope with additional work by means of other than extra staff.

- Anxiety to recruit staff in advance of the time when they are really needed.
- Over-elaboration of paperwork systems.
- Uncoordinated documentary systems leading to duplication of work.
- Wasteful or inefficient procedures.
- Ineffective supervision.
- Badly trained staff.

These problems are sufficiently common in most organizations to alert you to the need to take greater care in seeking justifications for existing levels of clerical staff as well as reasons for wanting more.

Managerial and professional staff
This is the most difficult area in which to produce satisfactory budgets. It is so much a matter of judgement, especially in technical and financial departments. Ratio-trend analysis is seldom helpful. Overmanning can result from any of the reasons mentioned above for clerical staff and a range of other factors:

1. Unclear definitions of what the function, department or individual is there to achieve.
2. Poor organization structures which create too many intermediary levels of management and supervision, each of which generates its own extra staff requirements as well as manufacturing work for others.
3. The multiplication of overstaffed head office departments, which again tend to create unnecessary work for themselves and others.
4. The tendency of some managers to 'empire build', either out of a genuine, if mistaken, feeling that their function needs to expand, or as a means of increasing their own prestige.

These tendencies can only be curbed if you subject each managerial post and support or service activity to rigorous scrutiny, to ensure not only that extra staff are fully justified, but also that the continued existence of the present establishment or even the function itself is necessary. There is no easy method of achieving this: all you can do is to ask questions about what is done, why it is done, what results are achieved and what contribution the activity makes to the organization. Finally, you should ask if the work could be done another way, with less people, by another department or not at all, without any detrimental effects on the company.

Translating budget forecasts into employment programmes

The human resource budget should not simply be a device to enable you to control the numbers employed. It should also provide essential information for planning recruitment or preparing programmes for reducing numbers.

Recruitment plans should aim to minimize the costs involved as well as providing the quantity and quality of staff required. Advertisements can be scheduled to obtain the benefit of reduced rates and an attempt can be made to smooth out peaks in the programme to avoid increasing the costs of staffing the personnel department.

Plans for reducing numbers should be made as far in advance as possible so that recruitment can be frozen and the reduction achieved by natural wastage.

PART III

Human Resource Systems

Introduction

Human resource management takes a corporate view. It can be defined as a total approach to the strategic management of a key resource which has to be the responsibility of the board, with advice from personnel specialists. Personnel management provides that advice and the services required to implement the plan.

Those services will take the form of various human resource systems or programmes which are designed to ensure that the organization gets the people it needs and appraises, rewards and looks after them properly. The main 'people programmes' are:

- *Recruitment management* – obtaining the resources required.
- *Performance management* – systematically appraising performance against defined criteria, reviewing progress to date and assessing potential for advancement and providing the information required for the administration of reward and career management programmes.
- *Reward management* – ensuring that people are rewarded in accordance with their contribution (paying for performance).
- *Career management* – providing the guidance, counselling and training needed to improve performance and develop potential.
- *Health and safety management* – maintaining a healthy and safe system of work.

9. Obtaining Human Resources

When you have decided how many and, broadly, what sort of people you want, you set about getting them by knowing:

- What you are looking for.
- Where to find them.
- How to attract them.
- How to choose them.
- How to clinch the deal.
- What to do with them when they start.

WHAT YOU ARE LOOKING FOR

Most of the people you recruit will probably be replacements and of course you know what you are looking for. But do you? One of the main reasons why people leave is because they should not have been selected in the first place. Mistakes are made because the duties and responsibilities of the job have not been properly analysed, neither has an adequate specification been prepared of what the job holder needs to know and be able to do.

For new jobs, the requirement to analyse the duties and to prepare job specifications based on this analysis is even more pressing. It is likely that only a superficial understanding of what the job is existed when the human resource plans were being prepared.

To know what you are looking for, you need to do three things:

1. Analyse the job, and then:
2. Prepare a job description.
3. Prepare a personnel specification.

Job analysis

Job analysis establishes what the tasks and duties of the job are. The information required covers:

- The job title.
- An organization chart showing at least the job title of the job holder's immediate superior and the job titles of the staff directly responsible to him.
- A definition of the overall purpose of the job.
- A list of the main tasks or duties that the job holder carries out.
- The initial dimensions of the job – sales turnover, size of budget, number of staff controlled, output or throughput etc.
- Any special equipment or tools used.
- Information on any special requirement to deal with people – inside or outside the organization.
- Special circumstances, such as travelling away from home, the likelihood of being transferred to another branch or location, unsocial hours, unpleasant or dangerous working conditions.

This information can be obtained by talking to the boss or the existing job holder, if feasible. Questionnaires are sometimes used, but most people are not very good at completing them and you still have to talk it over. It is, however, advisable to warn the person you are seeing in advance of what you will want to know, so that organization charts or any other data can be made available in time for the meeting.

Job descriptions

Job descriptions provide four pieces of information:

1. *The job title*: this should be as precise as possible about what the job is, without being over-elaborate. Try not to allow a proliferation of inflated titles such as director, manager or executive. They may impress other people, but they do not cut much ice within the organization and only serve to devalue jobs where the title means something.
2. *Basic organization*: the person to whom the job holder is responsible and the people responsible to him.
3. *Overall responsibility*: a succinct (one or two sentences) statement of what the job exists to do. It should be possible from this statement to distinguish it from other jobs in the organization and to lead naturally into a description of the main duties or principal accountabilities. For example, the statement of overall purpose for a divisional production director might read:

   The divisional production director is responsible for ensuring that the production commitments of the division are achieved in the quantities and qualities required and in accordance with predetermined programmes and cost budgets.

4. *Main activities*: the list of main activities, duties, principal accountabilities or responsibilities (which of these terms is used is immaterial) is the most important part of the job description. Each activity should represent a key element of the job for which the job holder can be held accountable and which requires specific knowledge or skills. Your aim should be to restrict the number of headings to six or seven so that the crucial aspects of the job can be highlighted. There may, however, be a number of related tasks that can be specified under each activity heading.

For example, the headings in a retail shop manager's job description might read: selling; display; merchandising; stock control; staff management and training. Under the 'selling' heading, there might be three related tasks which would be described as follows:

1. Greets customers and passes them to the appropriate sales assistant.
2. Ensures that customers are handled correctly by the sales assistant.
3. Sells direct to customers when necessary.

Activity descriptions indicate *what* is to be done. They should not attempt to spell out *how* it is done, although the outline in the job description may be expanded into a task analysis for training purposes, which goes into more detail so that the skills and knowledge required to do each task can be identified.

The three golden rules for writing activity definitions are:

1. The definition should be succinct but informative.
2. Each definition should be expressed in one sentence starting with an active functional verb, eg:
   - prepares regional sales forecasts;
   - checks quotations prepared by the sales department;
   - answers customer queries on deliveries.
3. The definitions should be set down in separate, numbered paragraphs to ease identification of the key areas and to assist in cross-referencing.

Figure 9.1 shows an example of a job description for a product manager in a marketing department.

Other uses for the job description

The job description is a basic tool of human resource management. It is essential not only because it provides vital data for recuitment purposes, but also because it provides key information for use in:

- Organization design and development.
- Human resource planning.
- Training.
- Management development.
- Performance reviews.
- Salary administration (job evaluation).

Job title - Product Manager
Responsible to - Product Group Manager
Responsible to him/her - Assistant Product Managers (2)
Overall responsibility Achieves contribution targets for product by developing and implementing plans, monitoring performance and initiating corrective action.
Main activities 1. Develops a long-range and competitive strategy for the product. 2. Prepares annual marketing plans and sales forecasts. 3. Works with advertising agencies to develop and implement promotional and advertising campaigns. 4. Stimulates interest and support for the product among the sales force and distributors. 5. Gathers continuous intelligence on the product's performance, customer and dealer attitudes and new problems and opportunities. 6. Initiates and tests product improvements to meet changing market needs.

Figure 9.1 *Sample job description*

Personnel specification

The personnel specification tells you six things:

1. The knowledge, skills and personal attributes needed to do the job. These may be classified either as essential or desirable.
2. The qualifications, experience and training which are likely to provide the knowledge and skills required. These may also be classified as essential or desirable.
3. Age limits, if any.
4. Prospects of promotion.

5. Features of the job – location, unsocial hours, travelling, working conditions, likelihood of transfer.
6. Terms and conditions of employment – basic pay, bonuses, pension, other fringe benefits, working hours, holidays, periods of notice etc.

The specification is used, together with the job description, first, as a basis for drafting advertisements or briefing recruitment consultants, second, to provide the criteria against which candidates can be assessed and third, as a source of the information which needs to be conveyed to candidates in interviews and offers of employment.

A personnel specification for a product manager might read as follows:

1. *Knowledge*:
   - *essential* – techniques of marketing planning, sales forecasting, product analysis, pricing, target marketing and marketing control;
   - *desirable* – techniques of marketing research, new product development and media planning.
2. *Skills*:
   - *essential* – numerate in the sense of being at ease in handling figures and basic statistical analysis, good on paper (report writing), high level of analytical ability;
   - *desirable* – managing and motivating people, persuasive (selling) skills.
3. *Qualifications*.
   - *essential* – graduate or equivalent;
   - *desirable* – first or second degree in business studies with emphasis on marketing, Member of Institute of Marketing.
4. *Training*:
   - *essential* (if no business or marketing qualification) – specialized short courses in marketing techniques, or evidence that he/she is familiar through reading or on-the-job training with basic concepts of marketing;
   - *desirable* – extended full- or part-time courses in marketing.
5. *Experience*:
   - *essential* – two years' experience after graduation as an assistant product or brand manager in a marketing department or an advertising agency;
   - *desirable* – experience in a FMCG (fast moving consumer goods) business, and/or experience in new product development and launches.
6. *Personal attributes*:

- *essential* – extrovert, an achiever, articulate, capable of working under pressure.
7. *Age limits*: 23 – 28.
8. *Promotion prospects*: effective product managers can normally expect promotion to product group manager within two years.
9. *Job features*: based in Central London, some UK travelling, occasional late-night, even weekend working (ie can be pressurized).
10. *Terms and conditions*:
    - *starting salary circa* £X,000 up to £Y,000 in special circumstances;
    - *salary range* £X,000-£Z,000;
    - *holiday* – five weeks;
    - *pension scheme* – non-contributory, contracted in;
    - *working week* – basic, 35 hours (9.30-5.30 Monday to Friday with one hour allowed for lunch);
    - *period of notice* – one month;
    - *expenses* – normal, including mileage allowance for using own car on business (NB no company car, allocation starts at product group manager level);
    - *luncheon vouchers* – £X per day;
    - *season ticket loan* – after six months' service.

WHERE TO FIND THEM

Internal candidates

You may believe that you already have the ideal candidate within your organization, possibly someone who has been groomed for promotion, but it would be wise to check your assumptions. Compare his or her qualifications with the specification. If they match, that is fine. If they do not fit exactly, think again. You may continue to feel that this is your best bet and, after all, promotion from within is a good thing, isn't it? If, however, a fresh look at the individual means that you have second thoughts, check to see if there is anyone else within the organization. You might want to stick to your first choice, but you will be more certain that you are right.

If no obvious choice springs to mind you should still consider an internal 'trawl', if you believe that there are any suitable people around who would be interested because the job will offer promotion, upgrading, wider experience, or just a change. You may know someone, or you can ask around, or look at the records. If your personnel records are computerized (and they should be in any but the smallest organization) you might be able to obtain a printout of people who have the basic qualifications for the job. This implies that the records store the sort of information you need for this purpose. If they don't, then the deficiency should be remedied.

If the trawl brings nothing worthwhile into the net, you can consider an internal advertisement. Many companies do this as a matter of policy in the interest of equal opportunity. This may be highly desirable, but it could be argued that if internal advertisements are mandatory and a manager is absolutely certain about who he wants, then advertising would be an empty gesture and might cause more frustration and disappointment than if an appointment had been made without going through this rigmarole. Alternatively, it could be felt that as there is no one suitable in the company, there would be no point in going through the futile and time-wasting process of advertising inside. The answer to this objection may be that no one can be absolutely certain in any sizeable organization that there are no suitable internal candidates and, in any case, everyone ought to be given the chance. This view has much merit, but there will be circumstances where an internal advertisement is a pointless exercise.

External sources

Even if you have internal candidates or advertise in the company, you may still feel that you have to extend your choice outside. The alternative sources are:

1. *Former employees*: approach them on a 'Will ye no come back again?' basis.
2. *Advertisements*: discussed in the next section.
3. *Government employment agencies* (in the UK): job centres for manual and junior clerical staff, the PER (Professional and Executive Recruitment) for managerial and professional staff.
4. *Private employment bureaux,* which deal with general secretarial, clerical or junior professional vacancies, or may specialize in such occupations or areas of business as computer personnel, accountants, graphic designers or publishing. They charge a fairly substantial fee, from 6 to 7 per cent to as high as 17.5 per cent, but save time and trouble and often have direct access to the most appropriate candidates.
5. *Selection or recruitment consultants,* who produce a short-list of candidates for you from advertisements (which may or may not mention the name of your firm) or from their lists of suitable candidates on file. They charge a fee which may be of the order of 15

to 20 per cent of the successful applicant's salary, and they also bill you for the costs of advertising and testing and for travelling and incidental expenses.

The advantage of a good firm is that it has expertise in analysing requirements and writing advertisements and in interviewing. It should also know about salary levels. You save time, although you have to pay for it, and you can, if you wish, remain anonymous so as not to upset your own employees. This sounds an undesirable motive, but there are occasions when employers want to explore the market for a new job without revealing all the details, including salary, to their existing staff.

You should consider the following points when choosing and using a selection consultant:

- whenever you can, use consultants with whom you are familiar and who have given you good service in previous assignments – they know you and your business;
- if you are starting from scratch, obtain recommendations from other users;
- establish which firms have specialist experience in your industry or for a particular occupation;
- check the advertisements of possible consultancies to give you a direct impression of their professionalism and the type and level of firms and jobs they deal with;
- make sure that you meet the consultant who is actually going to conduct the assignment. Check his experience. Assess his competence. If you don't like him, go elsewhere;
- once you have selected the selector, discuss with him the basis upon which he will carry out the assignment, including preparing specifications, advertising (agree a media plan detailing the paper or journals to be used), reporting on candidates, and the basis upon which the short-list will be drawn up. The consultant may simply hand over details of the short-listed candidates and leave you to carry out the final selection, but if you wish, he can sit in on the interviews to provide you with further advice – at a cost;
- clarify the basis upon which fees and expenses will be charged and get a prior quotation for the full cost or, if that is difficult, set a maximum figure. Make sure you know what the bill for advertising is going to be, otherwise you could get a nasty shock;
- use the consultant's expertise in drawing up the job description, defining the personnel specification and setting the remuneration levels, but don't allow him to persuade you to escalate the salary to an amount which would cause you embarrassment

within your firm when it is compared with what equivalent staff are paid. If you agree that the salary should be quoted as *circa* £X,000,make sure that both you and the consultant know what you mean. How far, if at all, will you go above that figure to attract an especially good candidate? What activity, if any, should you give the consultant to indicate that a higher salary is payable? It is best not to allow him – or yourself – to commit yourself to any fixed figure in advance; leave it to negotiation in the final stages. Neither should the consultant be drawn into detailed discussion in the early stages about terms and conditions of employment;

- obtain a written confirmation of your brief, together with copies of the agreed personnel specification and draft advertisements for you to approve (check remuneration details);

- finally, trust your consultant. Within reasonable limits, give him any sensitive information about your firm he needs to know, but clear with him in advance what he can tell the candidate.

6. *Executive search consultants* (head hunters) approach candidates direct having obtained their names by 'research' or through contacts. The blue-blooded ones with plush offices in Mayfair only deal with top jobs, but there are specialist agencies who cover more junior or professional vacancies. Head hunters are most useful when there is only a limited number of potential candidates, few of whom are likely to be seeking alternative employment. They can make direct approaches to people you or they know who are right for the job and they can also handle with discretion senior people who may not wish to come out into the open. Search fees can be as high as 50 per cent of the first year's salary, and results are not always guaranteed.

There are a number of reputable and well established search consultancies, but sharks and charlatans exist. The advice on choosing and using a consultant given above is equally applicable to head hunters.

7. *Schools*: schools can be approached direct through careers teachers. It is often worth cultivating local schools – arranging visits, providing holiday jobs or sponsoring events. You will create goodwill and possibly spot promising school leavers.

8. *Universities*: the big firms recruit large numbers of newly qualified graduates through the 'milk round' – visiting universities to interview candidates.

Companies which recruit from universities on a large scale produce glossy brochures and even video tapes. They work through the careers advisory services and employ specialists who are good at relating to students. If you only want one or two graduates in the UK you can advertise in the fortnightly 'Current Vacancies' list issued by the Central Services Unit in Manchester, or you can announce your vacancies on Prestel.

HOW TO ATTRACT THEM

Basic considerations

1. *Pay*: the first thing to do is to ensure that the remuneration package is attractive. This means paying the market rate unless the job or the company's reputation are good enough to persuade people to settle for less – and this is a rare event. You can find out what market rates are by studying advertisements for comparable jobs. Some people say that these rates are unreliable and, indeed, they may not reflect what is eventually paid. But you will be competing in the job vacancy pages against other firms, so you must take into account what they offer.

   There is no point in offering less that the average, except in the ultra-special circumstances referred to above. How far you go above the average depends on how badly you want to attract the best available candidates and the extent to which you need to compensate for any drawbacks in the job. When deciding on salary levels and other parts of the remuneration package you must also, of course, have regard to your internal scales so as not to upset relativities, unless there is a good reason for paying a premium to attract a top-rate external candidate.

   Check the salary you are offering against any information on salary levels you can obtain from published salary surveys (discussed in more detail in Chapter 11). Advice can also be obtained from the selection consultant, if you are using one.

2. *The job*: you are more likely to get someone good if the job, as described in the advertisement or at the interview, looks, sounds and *is* good from the points of view of interest, challenge and opportunity.

Advertising

You can use a specialist recruitment advertising agency, but if you are doing it yourself (and apart from the time it takes, there is a lot to be said for it) the following is a checklist of the points to which you need to pay attention:

1. *Set objectives*:
   - to attract response from suitable candidates;
   - to deter unsuitable candidates;
   - to create a favourable impression of you as an employer;
   - to enhance the reputation of your firm.
2. *Achieving objectives*: to obtain a good response from an advertisement you need to:
   - catch the *attention* of the people to whom it is addressed;
   - hold their *interest* so that your proposition is read thoroughly;
   - arouse *desire* for the opportunity offered;
   - stimulate *action* in the shape of response.
3. *Information content*: a potential employee will want the advertisement to provide him with answers to these questions about the job:
   - is the work interesting?
   - is it relevant to my qualifications and experience?
   - is the pay right?
   - will it advance my career?
   - is it secure?
4. *Creating the advertisement*:
   - catch attention with a bold headline which in a few words will make a potential applicant read on. Illustrations can help;
   - stimulate interest by describing the job in the first paragraph in a way which will make it personally rewarding;
   - create desire by mentioning opportunities for advancement early in the copy;
   - don't use up too much space describing the company. This is not primarily a public relations exercise. But do tell them where the job is located, and capitalize on a good location;
   - summarize the qualifications and experience. Aim reasonably high. If you understate your requirements you will undersell the job. But be specific; vague references to desirable characteristics such as initiative, judgement or ambition do not add much;
   - state age limits, but don't be too restrictive;
   - describe the remuneration package – salary, company car, pension scheme, relocation expenses etc. Concentrate on the key attractive elements. Quoting the salary as *circa* £X,000 gives you and the candidate room to manoeuvre; stating that the salary is 'up to' creates expectations which you might not want to fulfil;
   - stimulate action by telling them how to apply. You can ask them to write a letter of application or, and this often works well, ask them to write or telephone for an application form. If you are raiding a place for a particular category of staff employed locally, you can invite them to attend an informal interview in an hotel;

- use clear, simple, easy-to-read typography with plenty of white space so that it stands out on the page. Establish a 'house style' if you are advertising frequently;
- use display advertisements for important jobs. But semi-display, even classified ads can work well for more junior positions;
- use sufficient space in a display advertisement to ensure that it is not swamped by the other ads on the page. But space is expensive and excessively large advertisements are not necessarily cost-effective.

5. *Media selection*: choose media which have been successful in the past or are right for the particular vacancy. If you scan the pages of the 'quality' papers and the more popular press you will soon get a picture of which jobs to advertise where. Some papers have specialist sections, such as the *Guardian* for media jobs. Others go direct to the right audience – the *Financial Times* is appropriate for senior financial posts. The *Daily Telegraph* is a good general medium for managerial, professional and technical vacancies. Top jobs may be advertised in *The Times*, the *Sunday Times* or the *Observer*. Your local or evening paper is best for clerical and manual jobs. Journals are useful for specialist posts – *Campaign*, for example, is good for agency and marketing jobs. But circulation may be low and it might be advisable to use the journal as a back-up to a general medium. Up-to-date information on each medium is listed in the monthly *BRAD* (British Rate and Data).

6. *Budgeting*: as a rule of thumb, you may have to spend the equivalent of two to three weeks' wages for semi-skilled or skilled workers; over three weeks' pay for secretarial and clerical posts; and six to eight weeks' salary for managerial, professional and technical posts. The amount you spend will clearly depend on the extent to which you are in a buyer's or seller's market for the type of person you are looking for. Response analysis (see below) of previous advertisements will give you an idea of how much each reply and recruit will cost, but do not rely on data more than 12 months old.

7. *Response analysis*: to assist in budgeting and in analysing the performance of an advertisement, it is essential to analyse the response you get. Records should be kept for each insertion of the total cost, the number of replies, the number called for interview and the number of joiners (assuming there is more than one vacancy). This data can be used to produce these ratios:
- cost per reply (the basic ratio);
- cost per interview (an index of quality);
- cost per recruit;
- replies per joiner.

8. *Using a recruitment advertising agency*: an agency will be able to provide expert services on copywriting, advertising design and media selection. They are most useful if you are planning a major campaign or are expecting problems in attracting good candidates. Agencies rely for their income mainly on the commission they receive on the space they place with the media. Some agencies work on a fee basis, rebating their commission from the total fee.

HOW TO CHOOSE THEM

The process of choosing people consists of the following four stages, one of which, testing, is optional:

1. Sifting.
2. Interviewing.
3. Testing.
4. Obtaining references.

Sifting applications

Interviewing is a time-consuming process. Given the choice, you are not likely to want to see more than a dozen people for one vacancy, and if you could reduce this to half-a-dozen, so much the better. Assuming you have had a decent response to your advertisement, you have to sift the applications.

There are six questions you should answer when reading a letter, CV or application form:

1. Does the applicant meet the minimum criteria in the specifications for qualifications, experience and age range?
2. To what extent does the applicant's educational and work history indicate achievement and progression?
3. Are there any features in the applicant's career such as job hopping or mysterious gaps which arouse suspicion?
4. On the face of it, are the reasons given for leaving jobs convincing?
5. If the applicant is unemployed, how long has this lasted and what happened to the last job?
6. Is the letter of application or CV business-like, clear and readable? The more important the job, the greater the weight that should be given to this information. An incoherent, verbose or badly written letter suggests the possession of undesirable characteristics such as an untidy mind, an inability to communicate, or a couldn't-care-

less attitude. Don't reject someone who meets the specification in every respect, just because the letter is somewhat confused, but, other things being equal, a badly set out application may tip the balance against the candidate.

If you have received a lot of applications, you will need to classify them. Three categories are enough in the first sift: possibles, doubtfuls and outright rejects. Don't waste any time with the latter, there are always some no-hopers who are obviously unsuitable; clear them out of the way.

Unless you are in a desperate hurry, allow a week to go by and then carry out a second sift of the possibles and doubtfuls. This time, classify them into probables (the ones you want to call for interview), possibles (the ones you will hold for the present, pending the results of the first interviews) and rejects. Ideally, you should have six to twelve probables and as many possibles for one vacancy. Put the rest out of their misery straight away. As a rule of thumb, try and cover your probables by as many possibles.

When you have sifted twice, invite the probables for interview. Allow 30 minutes for a clerical or manual vacancy, and 60 minutes for a managerial post – possibly more at a really senior level. Try not to invite too many people on one day; a dozen clerical or manual workers or six managers is enough. If you try and do more you will be unable to do the tail-end candidates justice, and you could miss a good one. When scheduling interviews, bring in the best candidates first, allow some time between interviews (5–10 minutes) to collect your thoughts and write down your first impressions, and leave some empty slots in the day to allow you to rearrange dates or times.

At this stage you should send the applicant an application form if you have not already done so. The form should elicit all the information you need as a basis for the interview and making the final choice. This covers:

- Personal details – age, sex, marital status, children if any.
- Education.
- Qualifications and training.
- Job history – for each job, name of company, job title, job title of person to whom the applicant was responsible, starting and leaving dates, final salary or rate of pay and reason for leaving.
- Names of referees.

Interviewing

The best sort of interview is on a one-to-one or, at most, two-to-one basis. The final choice should be made by one person only – whoever is going to be the boss. He can be assisted by a personnel specialist who may carry out a preliminary sifting interview, only passing on suitable candidates for a final interview. If there is a fairly small list of people to be interviewed, the personnel specialist may sit with the line manager. Both approaches have their advantages and disadvantages.

Separate interviews could mean that more ground is covered and different facets of the candidate's qualifications and experience are exposed. The personnel specialist may concentrate on educational and job history and on explaining attitudes and motivation. The line manager may deal with the more technical aspects of the job and make his personal assessment of whether or not the candidate will fit into the department. However, separate interviews can be time wasting and inevitably overlap.

The advantage of joint interviews is that both interviewers are exposed to the same information and either of them can follow leads created in advance, and while one interviewer asks the questions the other can sit back and observe reactions. There is a lot to be said for this approach if there is no need to sift at the interview stage. Alternatively, a colleague of the manager can sit in at the preliminary personnel interview or alongside the manager.

As a general rule, using more than two interviewers at a time is counter-productive. The candidate becomes confused, it is difficult to get a natural flow of questions and, because each interviewer feels he has to have his say, leads are not followed up and the candidate is not given enough scope to express himself. Interviewing boards may be desirable, even necessary, in the civil service and local government for political reasons, but they are not an effective way of choosing people.

For the more routine or junior jobs, one interview or a pair of interviews in quick succession is usually enough. At more senior levels, a second interview is desirable to give all concerned another chance to get to know each other thoroughly; selecting someone for a job is a momentous decision and should not be undertaken too lightly.

Purpose
An interview is a conversation with a purpose. The purpose is to obtain information about the candidate so that you can assess his qualifications and personal qualities against the specification and thus make a prediction about his capacity to do the job. This purpose is achieved through a conversation, because by adopting a fairly informal, conversational approach, you are more likely to get the information you want.

Basic approach
The conversational approach is fundamental, but there are three other Cs to which you need to pay attention:

1. *Contact*: establish rapport as quickly as you can. You want the candidate to talk and thus to reveal all you need to know. People can talk themselves out of as well as into a job. A friendly opening is required, but this does not mean that you should not be prepared to toughen up later if you want really to pin down the candidate about what he knows or can do.
2. *Content*: make sure that you cover all the ground by systematically reviewing every relevant aspect of the candidate's education, training and career. Get the facts, but also try to get to know something about his motivation, his attitude to work, his ability to communicate and the way he gets on with people - bosses, colleagues and subordinates.
3. *Control*: your conversation should be controlled to get the information you need within the time available. Control yourself as well as the candidate. Don't talk too much, and keep him to the point.

Interview plan
The best way to get what you want is to determine in advance how you are going to tackle the interview. Read the application form again before you see the candidate. Decide on the questions you need to ask to clarify job history, to explore his depth of understanding of what he does and knows, and to test his ability to cope with the demands of the job for which he is being interviewed.

Also decide how you are going to plan the interview. A typical and logical method is the biographical interview, starting with education and qualifications and then, if applicable, covering each job in turn, concentrating on the most recent jobs. Time should be allowed for general questions about personal circumstances and interests and to tell the candidate about the company and the job. He should be given the opportunity to ask questions; the quality of his questions could be revealing.

It is usually advisable to leave the detailed description of the job until after you have interviewed the candidate: there is no point in spending a lot of time telling an unsuitable individual all about a job you are not going to offer him.

Interviewing techniques
The following list summarizes the things you should and should not do
to conduct a successful interview:

Dos:

- Ensure you know what you are looking for – read the specification.
- Decide in advance on any technical questions you want to ask to test
  the candidate's knowledge.
- Prepare, by reading the application form again and deciding how
  you want to plan the interview – the order in which you want to
  cover the ground and the particular questions you want to ask.
- Follow your plan and ensure you go over every point.
- Get the candidate to talk freely – offer open invitations for him to
  respond, such as: 'Tell me how you got on at school', 'What do you
  find most rewarding about your current job?' You don't want 'yes'
  or 'no' responses; they tell you next to nothing.
- Ask questions which will give you some idea about the candidate's
  motivation and ambitions, such as: 'What made you study that
  particular subject?', 'What made you decide to do. . .?', 'Why did you
  make that move?', 'How do you think you have progressed so far in
  your career?'
- Give the candidate the opportunity to reveal his strengths: 'What
  was your proudest moment at school?', 'What would you say have
  been your major achievements in your present job?'
- Try to identify any weaknesses or failures. This is not easy; the
  candidate will do his best to disguise, avoid or gloss over them. All
  you can do is to press hard to find out the real reasons why he has
  hopped from job to job, or why he left his last job after only a few
  months. If, for example, his explanation for leaving his last job is 'I
  couldn't get on with my boss'; probe. Ask him to tell you, with
  examples, what actually went wrong. Whose fault was it? Ask him
  open-ended questions such as: 'What sort of problems have you had
  to deal with?'
- Ensure that any gaps in the candidate's record are filled up. A 12-
  month space between jobs might have been spent back-packing
  around Asia, but could have been spent in gaol.
- Look for patterns: continuous progression from success to success,
  or a series of short spells in jobs. Anyone can be unlucky enough to
  be made redundant or even fired on one occasion. If it happens
  more than once, you need to watch out. He may have gone on being
  unfortunate, but it could occur again if he joins your firm.
- Look for evidence of the skills you are seeking. For example,
  positions of responsibility at school or university, if you want a

future manager; making things, if you want a craftsman.

- Seek any evidence you can obtain on motivation. Success at school, university, professional training or in his career is the best guide. You can also find out quite a lot about the degree to which a person is motivated by asking about interests outside education or work.

    The sort and range of interests will tell you something about the candidate, but the depth at which he pursues them will tell you a lot more. If, for instance he says he reads, find out what he reads, how much he reads and if he can talk intelligently about his current reading.

    One indicator of motivation is when someone triumphs over disadvantages such as a relatively poor home. On the other hand, a lack of motivation might be indicated if someone has not made the most of his natural advantages.

Don'ts:

- Avoid jumping to conclusions on limited evidence. First impressions can be misleading. Interviewers often seize on one desirable characteristic, such as a lively manner, and allow this reaction to obscure manifold weaknesses. There are plenty of con-artists about in interview rooms as well as on the streets. The candidate, if he wants the job, is out to make a good impression. He will present himself as well as he can and put a bold front over any failings. Your task is to penetrate behind the facade. Avoid indulging in what is known as the 'halo effect', which means letting one superficially attractive characteristic overshadow other less desirable ones. 'The halo is only nine inches away from the noose', as Sir Peter Parker said.
- Don't ask leading questions – those that clearly indicate the answer you want. If you ask someone 'Do you think you are good at so- and-so?' he is almost certain to answer yes, which does not get you very far. You need factual evidence which emerges from questions about achievements and experience and is not simply a matter of following your lead with an assertion of what he believes you would like to hear.
- Try your best not to dominate the interview – the candidate must be able to talk freely. Limit your contribution to well prepared, succinct and open questions and continue by means of encouraging grunts.
- Don't allow the interview to drift – keep control and keep within your time limit.

Assessing candidates

You should assess candidates against the headings included in the specification:

- Knowlege.
- Skills.
- Qualifications.
- Training.
- Experience.
- Personal attributes.

A simple form can be drawn up with these headings, and for each one you can grade the candidate as follows:

A = exceeds specification
B = meets specification
C = does not meet specification

Anyone with a C in one or more critical areas is eliminated unless there is an overwhelming case for making an exception because of a particularly strong showing in another important area. For example, someone may not have the required qualifications but wins hands down on experience.

The job should not necessarily go to the candidate with the highest number of As or the best test scores. He could be over-qualified, and this could lead to frustration and ineffectiveness. However, this objection could be waived if there is plenty of scope for expanding responsibilities or for promotion.

Some interviewers attempt to weigh each heading by allocating points scores, but his gives a spurious impression of accuracy. Once you have established through the interview and any tests you may administer that a candidate has the required basic qualifications and experience, you are exercising judgement.

Your final choice between two equally well-qualified candidates may be governed by their personal attributes. You have to believe that the candidate will 'fit' into the organization and that you and your colleagues will be able to work with him. This is where subjectivity creeps in. Perhaps it should not, but in the real world we want people working in our organization with whom we think we will get along. You must eliminate prejudice when assessing candidates, and this includes, as the law requires, prejudices against race or sex. But if you genuinely feel, other things being equal, that one candidate will fit better than the others, then he gets the job, although your final decision may be delayed until you have checked references.

Testing

It is generally acknowledged that the interview alone can be an inefficient method of selecting people. Interviewers are sometimes prejudiced or they can fail to get the evidence they need, either because their basic techniques are inadequate or because, through poor technique again, they allow candidates to pull the wool over their eyes. At an interview, the only evidence you have on what a candidate knows or can do, or what sort of person he is, derives from the information the candidate gives you (which could be, and often is, biased or misleading), plus your own observations. Can you really say that you have all you need to know about someone who may work with you for years after a 60-minute conversation?

Although tests cannot replace an interview, they can, if properly prepared and administered, provide additional unbiased evidence. The main types of tests that can be used are:

1. *Intelligence tests*: these are the familiar tests which attempt to measure intelligence, especially reasoning power. The most common type produces an intelligence quotient (IQ), which is the ratio of the mental age achieved by the individual and the norm for the population as a whole, which is taken as 100. Thus an IQ of 125 indicates that the individual's intelligence is 25 per cent above the average, while an IQ of 75 indicates intelligence 25 per cent below the average.

   Extensive research has shown that intelligence is distributed across the whole population in accordance with the normal bell shaped curve of distribution, as illustrated in Figure 9.2. Some

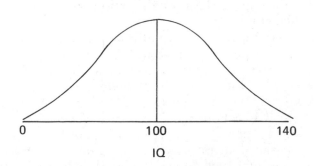

Figure 9.2 *A normal curve*

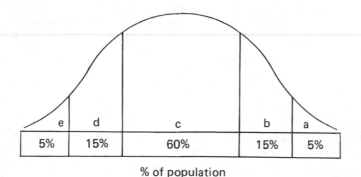

% of population

Figure 9.3 *Intelligence gradings*

intelligence tests do not measure IQ as such, but attempt to grade people into different divisions of the normal curve of distribution of intelligence for the population as a whole or a particular population, such as that of university graduates. A typical grade structure is shown in Figure 9.3.

2. *Attainment tests*: these measure abilities or skills that have already been acquired by training or experience. A typing test is the most typical example. It is easy to find out how many words a minute a typist can type and compare that with the standard required for the job.

3. *Aptitude tests*: aptitude tests are designed to predict the potential an individual has to perform a job or specific tasks within a job. They cover such areas as clerical aptitude, numerical aptitude, mechanical aptitude and dexterity. They may come in the form of well-validated single tests, or as a battery of tests developed by test agencies such as, in the UK, Saville and Holdsworth Ltd.

4. *Personality tests*: personality tests attempt to assess the type of personality possessed by the applicant in terms of traits (styles of behaviour, such as aggressiveness or persistence) or types (features which characterize an individual, such as extraversion or introversion). Personality tests should be treated with caution. They can provide some insight into an individual but they need to be validated by a thorough comparison of test results with subsequent behaviour.

To be useful, tests must satisfy two requirements. First, they must be valid in the sense that they measure what they are supposed to measure and

161

provide an indication of future behaviour. Second, they must be reliable in that they consistently produce the same results in similar circumstances.

Tests are useless unless they are validated by comparing the results achieved in the test with actual behaviour. This should be done scientifically so that norms can be established for evaluating test results. Thus, if it is shown that a job requires above average intelligence, only those whose test results lie in the upper quartile would be considered eligible. The same applies to aptitude and attainment tests. If there is inadequate correlation between test results and subsequent performance, the test becomes suspect. Before introducing a test, it is often worthwhile to administer it to existing staff whose performance has been measured so that the test results and actual achievements can be compared and realistic norms defined.

Tests can be useful for less senior jobs, where norms for intelligence, attainments or aptitudes can easily be determined. They are more difficult to apply at higher levels. Some people say that personality tests can provide valuable insights. This may be so, if they are the right tests, but their results should always be regarded as complementary to the other evidence you obtain from the application form and by the interview. Tests cannot supplant this information.

References

It is up to you to form your own opinion about the merits of a candidate. You cannot rely upon the possibly subjective views of someone else. What you can and should do, however, is to check with the present employer, and maybe the previous one as well, that the facts as given by the candidate are correct – job, length of service, rate of pay or salary (people have been known to exaggerate) and reasons for leaving, if applicable. You can also ask the key question, 'Would you re-employ?', but you will not always get a true answer. Any question asking directly or indirectly for an opinion about the ability of an individual to do a job with your company will as likely as not get a bland reply. People do not always like to commit themselves or damage someone's future prospects and, although references are privileged if they are factually correct and unmalicious, employers are worried about the possibility of an action for libel or slander. Because it is generally felt that it is difficult to make actions for slander stick, you are more likely to get a truthful reply if you get your reference over the telephone.

HOW TO CLINCH THE DEAL

The first thing to do is to sort out the pay. This presents no problem if there is a fixed rate for the job, but where there is some flexibility, you may have to negotiate around the *'circa'* figure quoted in your advertisement or the initial interview. If you do not offer at least the market rate as established by your research when preparing the job specification, you are not likely to get anyone worth having. You may decide to go above this level if the candidate is really good – but be aware of the danger of upsetting internal relativities and causing alarm, despondency and even anger among existing employees.

Your offer letter should deal with the main points that have to be covered in a contract of employment, namely:

- Job title.
- Starting date.
- Rates of pay and allowances and methods and intervals of payment.
- Hours of work.
- Holiday arrangements.
- Sick pay (if any).
- Pension arrangements.
- Length of notice.

STARTING ARRANGEMENTS

It is important to ensure that new employees get off to a good start. You will have spent quite a lot of money on obtaining them; why waste it by creating a bad impression?

Starters should be given all the information they need about the company, the facilities available to them (canteen, recreational, medical etc) and methods of payment. They should be shown round their department and some time should be spent in explaining how their job fits into the organization.

They may be no more than a cog in a large machine but they will be much better motivated if they appreciate the important part their cog plays.

Induction training should be arranged to ensure that the new employee knows exactly what is expected of him and can quickly master what he has to do.

New employees should be followed up before too long to ensure that they are settling down and have received adequate training. A formal review should take place after a few months when, if the employee is not performing adequately, steps can be taken in good time to warn him that there are problems. Guidance can then be given on what he needs to do to overcome them. This formal review will also provide a check on the effectiveness of the selection procedure.

10. Performance Management

Human resource management is very much concerned with excellence. This means the motivation and development of human resources so as to make a major contribution to the achievement of the organization's strategic objectives. The aim is to create a performance management system which starts from an assessment of how people are performing in their jobs, so that information is obtained as a basis for planning and implementing coaching, training, further experience or self-development programmes which will improve the results achieved by individuals and the organization as a whole.

Performance management is based on the information obtained from an appraisal or performance review system. There is, however, no other aspect of managing human resources which is generally done so badly as appraisal. Superficial and prejudiced judgements are made about individuals, who are left completely in the dark as to whether they are thought to be doing a good, bad or indifferent job. This inevitably leads to demotivation, distress or continuing poor performance. Given the opportunity, most people want to improve, as long as they feel there is something in it for them as well as for the organization, but an inadequate approach to performance management does not give them this chance. Both they and the company suffer.

There is a need to improve performance management techniques in almost any organization. This chapter therefore sets out to describe:

1. The purposes of appraisal.
2. How these purposes can be achieved.
3. Appraisal techniques.
4. The benefits that result from effective performance management.

PURPOSE OF APPRAISAL

Appraisal has three purposes:

1. To help improve performance by identifying strengths and weaknesses and by getting things done which will develop the former and overcome the latter.
2. To identify those with potential for greater responsibility, now or in the future, and to provide guidance on what should be done to ensure that this potential is realized.
3. To assist in deciding on pay increases which fairly equate the level of reward with the level of performance.

Appraisal is, or should be, a continuous process, but it is necessary from time to time to carry out a stock-taking exercise which reviews performance and progress over a period of time, so that a more comprehensive story can be built up to form the basis for considered action.

The starting point is the performance review, which poses three questions:

1. What has actually been achieved during the period against what was expected to be achieved?
2. What are the factors that influenced the level of achievement? These could relate to the personal efforts or abilities of the individual concerned, or to external factors beyond his direct control.
3. What needs to be done to improve performance?

The performance review leads to the potential review, which should answer two questions:

1. What potential has this individual to advance beyond his present level of responsibility?
2. What needs to be done to ensure that he fulfils his potential – by the company, his manager and himself?

Finally, the outcomes of the performance and potential reviews provide guidance on pay increases. Some people argue against linking performance reviews directly to pay because, they say, the financial factor outweighs the more important performance improvement considerations. But if, as you must, you believe in linking pay to performance, then this connection cannot be avoided. To minimize the risk of inhibiting an open discussion about performance, many firms carry out the salary review some weeks or months later than the performance review and, in effect, update the earlier assessment when deciding on the award.

THE APPRAISAL PROCESS

The appraisal process should deal so far as possible with objectively observed facts rather than subjective opinions. The aim is to get agreement between the boss and his subordinate on what the latter has achieved and what he needs to do to improve his performance. Such agreement is more likely to occur if the discussion is based on comparing agreed results with agreed targets or standards of performance. It is unreasonable to criticize someone for not achieving something which he was unaware he had to achieve. No one likes being criticized; it is only accepted and acted upon if it is felt to be fair – and it will only be considered fair if the individual fully accepts that he has not achieved standards which had previously been agreed by him as reasonable and attainable.

The appraisal procedure

A 'results-oriented' appraisal procedure fits in with the concept of accountable management discussed in Chapter 4. It requires the manager and his subordinate to hold joint discussions with a view to agreeing at each stage:

1. The overall purpose of the job.
2. The major tasks that have to be carried out to achieve that purpose. These tasks are sometimes called the key result areas or the principal accountabilities. They should be limited to seven or eight if possible.
3. For each task, the objectives to be achieved over a period defined as:
   - *targets* – results which can be quantified in such terms as profit, sales turnover, output or cost per unit of output;
   - *standards* – qualitative statements, in areas where quantitative targets cannot be set, of what has to be continuously achieved for the task to be well done. The statement completes the sentence: 'The standard of performance required for this task will have been achieved if...'
   - *special tasks or projects* – specific things that have to be carried out to a defined standard and within a stated period of time.
4. The results that have been achieved; comparing these with previously agreed targets, standards or special tasks, identifying the reasons for success or failure and agreeing the steps that should be taken to improve performance.
5. Revised objectives for the next review period.
6. The outcome of the actions agreed at stage 4 and any further actions required.

Appraisal system

The appraisal procedure outlined above should be carried out as informally as possible, using the minimum of paperwork. The original management by objectives movement, which is the basis of this approach, became discredited because of the weight of paper it used and the time it took to launch and administer. The work of agreeing responsibilities, setting objectives and reviewing results is part of the natural process of management; it should not be elaborated into a ritual.

The only pieces of paper you need are:

1. One sheet stating the overall purpose and listing the seven or eight main tasks, each described as succinctly as possible. This will need to be updated from time to time.
2. One sheet which lists the agreed targets, standards and projects. This is updated regularly at the beginning of each review period.
3. One sheet which records the results of the performance review. This should be limited to only four headings:
   - comments on results achieved;
   - comments on the strengths and weaknesses in performance which contributed to the results;
   - a statement of agreed actions on the part of the individual – specific things to be done to improve his performance by himself, or by his manager, who can provide coaching or arrange further experience or training;
   - a note by the manager on the extent to which the individual has potential and what needs to be done about it.

These pieces of paper are for the use of the manager and the individual concerned. They should not be lost in the machinery of some personnel department system. It is, however, desirable to extract information from the review sheet for company use, which will indicate any general training needs and list those with potential for promotion.

BENEFITS OF PERFORMANCE MANAGEMENT

Performance management ensures that managers and their subordinates are aware of what needs to be done to improve performance. It leads to performance-related training where every aspect of the programme is designed to satisfy a particular training need – a strength to be developed or a weakness to be overcome.

Performance management provides feedback so that people know where they stand, where they ought to be going and how they are going to get there. It can be linked to performance-related pay where the rewards are clearly dependent on the results achieved.

11. Reward Management

Reward management is essentially about designing, implementing and maintaining pay systems which help to improve organizational performance. To do this, the systems have to provide for competitive and equitable pay levels and structures and to ensure that rewards are linked explicitly to contribution, performance and potential.

The emphasis today is on paying for performance in order to achieve productivity through people. This theme was emphasized by Rosabeth Kanter when she wrote in the *Harvard Business Review* (March-April 1987):

> Status, not contribution, has traditionally been the basis for the numbers on employees' paychecks. Pay has reflected where jobs rank in the corporate hierarchy – not what comes out of them. Today this system is under attack. More and more senior executives are trying to turn their employees into entrepreneurs – people who earn a direct return on the value they help create, often in exchange for putting their pay at risk. In the process, changes are coming into play that will have revolutionary consequences for companies and their employees.

WHAT YOU MUST ACHIEVE

Objectives

You have to create and manage a pay or reward structure which will attract, retain and motivate the people you want. To do this, your reward system has to be:

1. *Externally competitive*: you must match market rates or you will certainly not be able to attract good quality staff. You will also find it difficult to retain them, unless working for your firm provides other benefits that money alone will not buy.
2. *Internally equitable*: your reward system must not only be fair, it

must be *felt* to be fair. There is nothing more likely to demotivate someone than knowing that other people are paid more for doing the same job, or worse, paid more for doing a less responsible job. If extra money is given for merit, it must be seen to be well deserved.

3. *Able to provide rewards which are commensurate with performance*: money is the most effective motivator, even if it is not the only one and its impact is not necessarily long lasting, as was seen in Chapter 5.

Achieving the objectives

To achieve these objectives, you need to:

- Understand the factors that affect pay levels.
- Know how to get reliable information on market rates.
- Know how to evaluate jobs in order to achieve an equitable pay structure.
- Understand the different wage systems you can operate.
- Be able to build and maintain a salary structure.
- Introduce and manage a system of pay administration which achieves consistency and economy in operation.

FACTORS AFFECTING PAY LEVELS

It can be said that a job is worth what the market says it is worth, but this is only a half-truth. Market forces, as influenced by supply and demand factors, are indeed important - if you are in competition for staff you must pay competitive rates. What you must also do, however, is pay what you think the job is worth to you.

The external factor of market rates and the internal need to provide rewards according to the contribution the job and the job holder make to the company are primary influences on pay levels, but there is another factor - union pressure leading to negotiated pay settlements. Their level is strongly affected by market rates, the movement of which is determined by inflation and the pressure of supply or demand for the category of labour concerned. Pay settlements, however, are also governed by the relative strengths of the employer and the trade union, and these will be influenced by the financial position of the firm and the state of the economy.

The three forces of market rates, internal value and trade union pressures exert different levels of pressure at different times and in different situations. One of the biggest problems you can meet in maintaining a competitive and equitable pay system is the reconciliation of these forces. It is all too easy to bow to market pressures and bring in someone at the only rate that will attract him; but this can so easily result in people already doing comparable jobs in the company being paid less than the newcomer, which can be a major cause of dissatisfaction. You will probably be forced to compromise.

You can, of course, try to resist paying excessive market rates, but if you are desperate for someone, this will be hard. Alternatively you can ensure that your internal rates keep pace with the market – highly desirable, but potentially expensive. It is possible to reduce the risk of being held to ransom by external candidates by trying your best to develop people inside your company and promote from within. You can then take advantage of the fact that for many jobs there is a sort of internal inertia which makes people unwilling to take the risk of a move or to unsettle themselves by vacating their comfortable rut, unless they receive an offer they cannot refuse.

This inertia partly compensates for the lag that exists between internal and market rates in even the best-run systems. You can take advantage of it by maintaining your rates at a level high enough to force a competitor to pay well above the odds for anyone who is likely to be in demand. You will not prevent apparently unrefusable offers being made but there will be fewer of these for your people to accept – and even if they are tempted, the more cautious ones may be suspicious that the excessive pay is being offered by a hire and fire company and the risks are therefore too great.

There are, of course, always some occupations where the pressures of market demands are so fierce that you must keep pace with market rates as closely as possible. Examples include qualified accountants, computer staff, exchange dealers, city analysts, fast-moving consumer goods marketing people, and top secretaries. For these categories, you may be forced to recognize the inevitable and create market rate pay structures which acknowledge that some jobs have to be paid more than strict conditions of internal equity require because of external considerations. Clearly, if you do this it is particularly important to ensure that you get accurate information on market rates, as described in the next section.

PAY SURVEYS

You can obtain information on market rates from the following sources:

1. *Advertisements*: treat job advertisements with some suspicion because the jobs may not be comparable or rates might be misleading and, to a degree, they feed off one another, generating an inflationary spiral. But these are the rates you have to compete against if you advertise for staff, and these are the external levels of

pay that your own staff can most easily become aware of. Any advertising firm or marketing department knows that when *Campaign* is circulated, the most heavily thumbed pages are those containing the job ads.

2. *Consultants and agencies*: if you seek help from a recruitment consultant, a head hunter or an agency, they will advise you on what you have to pay. And they should know because they are in the business of keeping in touch with market rates; but they can mislead by exaggerating what you have to pay. The less scrupulous ones (a minority) may do this because it makes their life easier. For the best of reasons, as they see them, they may encourage clients to pay at the upper end of the scale to get a good response.

3. *Applicants*: if you advertise regularly you can get some idea of the rates paid elsewhere from what people say they are being paid. Caution, however, is necessary. Rates can be inflated.

4. *Published surveys*: there are a number of published surveys of management salaries such as, in the UK, Inbucon, Reward and Monks Publications. They rely upon information obtained from companies using standard job descriptions or from company reports. They will give a range quoting the arithmetic average or median (the mid-point in the range) and the upper and lower quartile figures (the rates which are respectively, three-quarters and a quarter of the way up the range). Tables are given showing the rates for different sizes of companies measured by turnover or number of employees, also for different industries and locations. The surveys also give details of fringe benefits such as company cars and pension schemes and information on bonus payments as well as base salaries.

   Special surveys are also produced for professional staff such as computer personnel, accountants and personnel managers.

   As long as a reasonable number of companies participate, published surveys give a good indication of the spread of market rates for particular jobs. Their major disadvantage is that you can never be sure that you are comparing like with like. A marketing manager in one firm can have a completely different range of responsibilities from one in another, even if it is in a similar industry and the firm is the same size.

5. *'Salary club' surveys*: a salary or pay club is a group of companies, probably in the same industry, which regularly exchanges information on rates of pay and fringe benefits. A well-run survey bases its comparisons on agreed job descriptions which, although they have to be generalized, provide you with a better chance of comparing like with like than the published surveys.

6. *Individual surveys*: you can initiate surveys yourself, with other companies whom you ask to give information on a reciprocal basis. Because these are one-off enquiries, you may not get the same range of data as from a club, and it may be difficult to agree job descriptions. More and more companies are now subscribing to published or private surveys and are unwilling to spend the time required to participate in individual surveys; but if you have the time and can persuade others to help, your own survey can provide you with highly relevant information.

You can use any one or a combination of these. The more important it is to get accurate information, the more the need to go to additional sources. A combination of a quick look at job advertisements, an opinion from a consultant and a glance at a public or private survey will give you a pretty good idea of the range of market rates. But it will not give you *the* market rate, because there is no such thing. All you will obtain is a range, and you must decide where you want to be in that range.

It is at this point that you may have to decide on what is sometimes called your 'pay posture' is to be. This is where you want your rates to fall compared with market rates. Do you want to be ahead of the market, ie pay at the upper quartile? This may be desirable, but it is expensive, and if everyone does it (and a lot of firms declare this as their aim) it is a somewhat inflationary device.

Alternatively, you may decide to do no more than match market levels, which means setting the median figure as your target rate. You may allow yourself flexibility to pay more to get or keep the above average person, or less if you are recruiting someone without the required experience whom you intend to train up to the level of effectiveness you want him to achieve.

No firms deliberately set their sights at below market rates, although they may allow themselves to slide into that position, from which they will have to extricate themselves if they find they can neither attract nor retain staff.

JOB EVALUATION

Aims

Job evaluation attempts to compare the relative intrinsic worth or value of jobs within an organization. It tries to establish a hierarchy of jobs, often placed within a job grade structure to which pay levels are attached. The rates of pay may be determined or at least strongly influenced by market rates or by negotiations. But within this context, job evaluation aims to provide guidance on internal relativities and differentials.

In a sense, every time you say to yourself that job A is worth more to the company than job B you are carrying out a form of job evaluation. Your decision could be largely subjective or instinctive and it will be influenced by historical factors and your own gut feelings. To reduce the danger of entirely subjective judgements, there is much to be said for an analytical approach which at least begins with a factual description of what the job entails.

Approach

The starting point to job evaluation is job analysis, as described in Chapter 9. This tells you what is done and provides a basis for comparison, because job evaluation is essentially a comparative process. What you are doing when you evaluate a job is to compare what you think it is worth with what you think other jobs are worth. The value or worth of a job is fundamentally the contribution which that job makes to achieving the objectives of the company. Because that contribution cannot be measured in absolute terms, you have to rely on comparative statements of what the job involves and of the results it is expected to achieve.

The job analysis leads to a description of what work is done, as in a job description produced for a selection procedure. Further analysis is required for job evaluation purposes to identify the degree to which various characteristics or factors which distinguish relative job values are present. There are many different varieties of job evaluation, which use various factors. The basic factors, however, tend to be:

1. *Responsibility*: the responsibilities of a job are the particular obligations that have to be assumed by anyone who carries out the job. Responsibility requires the exercise of discretion in making decisions which commit the use of the organization's resources. It is measured by reference to the scope or size of the job, the impact it makes on end results, the amount of authority the job holder has to make decisions, and the degree of freedom he has to act (the extent to which his work is supervised).
2. *Know-how*: the extent to which the job holder has to analyse, evaluate and innovate to solve problems.
3. *Complexity*: the range of tasks to be carried out and the variety of problems to be solved.

Job evaluation schemes

The main types of job evaluation schemes and their advantages and disadvantages are summarized below:

Scheme	Characteristics	Advantages	Disadvantages
Market rate evaluation	Jobs graded by reference to market rate data and direct comparisons with jobs at or near the same level within the organization.	Realistic, practical, straightforward and quick.	Market rate information may be difficult to obtain or inaccurate.
Ranking	Whole job comparisons are made to place them in order of importance.	Easy to apply and understand.	No defined standards of judgement – differences between jobs are not measured.
Job classification	Job grades are defined and jobs are slotted into the grades by comparing the whole job description with the grade definition.	Simple to operate and standards of judgement are provided in the shape of the grade definitions.	Difficult to fit complex jobs into one grade without using excessively elaborate grade definitions.
Points	Separate factors are scored to produce an overall points score for the job.	The analytic process of considering separate defined factors provides for objectivity and consistency in making judgements.	Complex to install and maintain – judgement is still required to rate jobs in respect of different factors.

Your choice will depend on the size and complexity of the organization, the types of job to be evaluated, the time and resources available and the extent to which the scheme has to be 'sold' to staff. Because all organizations are different in these respects, it is not possible to be categoric in laying down what scheme should be used.

In general, however, the market rate evaluation approach is suitable when quick and acceptable results are required, in situations where reasonably accurate market rate data can be obtained. The gradings resulting from this approach can be checked by carrying out a simple ranking exercise and, if it is felt that this would be helpful for future evaluations, the grades evolved in the scheme can be broadly defined by reference to the jobs allocated into them.

Ranking is a useful method if a wide range of jobs has to be covered quickly. It is best adopted, however, in combination with other approaches, either to confirm the gradings produced as a result of a market rate evaluation or as a preliminary exercise in developing a job classification scheme.

Job classification schemes are generally most suitable where a quick and simple approach is wanted for clerical workers. They have their uses for higher level jobs, however, where it is felt that an analytical points scheme is inappropriate but some guide for grading jobs is still required. In these circumstances, it is best to define the grades after completing a market rate evaluation and an overall ranking exercise.

Points schemes can be used in complex situations where it is felt that only a highly analytical approach would provide an acceptable basis for an evaluation. Their elaborate nature may make them difficult to understand, but if it is thought that the staff affected by job evaluation are going to be more favourably impressed by the sheer quantity of time and trouble involved in introducing a scheme, then the costs of a points scheme may well be justified.

Job evaluation programme

A job evaluation programme consists of the eight stages shown in Figure 11.1.

Stage 1 is the preliminary stage in which information is obtained about present arrangements, decisions are made on the need for a new scheme or revision of an existing scheme and a choice is made of the type of scheme to be used.

Stage 2 is the planning stage when the programme is drawn up, the staff affected are informed, arrangements are made as required for setting up joint working parties and the sample of jobs to be analysed is selected.

Stage 3 is the analysis stage when information is collected about the sample of bench-mark jobs as a basis for the internal and external evaluation.

Stage 4 is the internal evaluation stage when the jobs are ranked by means of the chosen evaluation scheme and graded, usually on a provisional basis pending the collection of market rate data, except where a job classification scheme is used to slot jobs into an existing job grade structure.

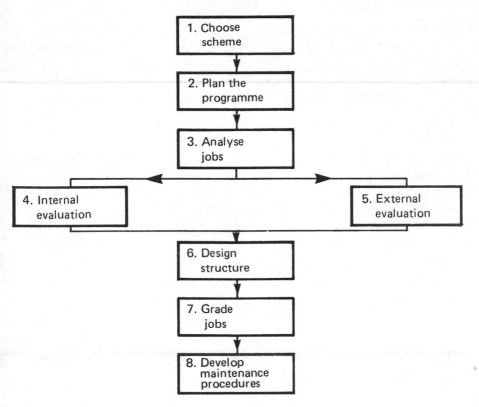

Figure 11.1 *Job evaluation programme*

Stage 5 is the external evaluation stage when information is obtained on market rates.

Stage 6 is the stage in which the salary structure is designed. (The different types of pay structure and the factors to be considered in developing a structure are dealt with in the next section.)

Stage 7 is the grading stage in which the jobs are slotted into the pay structure.

Stage 8 is the final stage in which the procedures for maintaining the salary structure are developed so that salary levels can be adjusted in response to inflationary pressures by means of general cost of living increases, new jobs can be graded into the structure, and existing jobs can be regraded as their responsibilities or market rates change.

SALARY STRUCTURES

A salary structure consists of the salary levels for single jobs or groups of jobs. In many smaller companies, the structure is no more than the set of salaries paid. Such arrangements have the advantage of flexibility and can work well as long as care is taken in fixing and progressing salaries. In larger companies, or where there is thought to be a need to exert careful control of salary levels, graded structures are more common.

Graded salary structures

A graded salary structure consists of a sequence of salary ranges or bands, each of which has a defined maximum and minimum. It is assumed that all the jobs allocated into a range are broadly of equal value, although there will be a system of salary progression (see below) which will mean that the salaries of individuals in a job will advance through the range for that job, in line with merit or service or a combination of the two.

A typical graded salary structure will look like Figure 11.2. The main features of such a structure are:

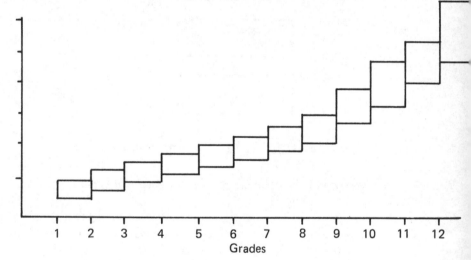

Figure 11.2 *Graded salary structure*

- The salary brackets are wide enough to progress salaries in relation to performance and in accordance with the level of the job. At junior levels, the top of the range could be 15 to 20 per cent above the lower limit. At managerial levels, the range could vary between 35 and 60 per cent, but the most typical width is 50 per cent.
- There is a differential of between 15 and 25 per cent between the mid-points of adjacent bands, to provide adequate scope for rewarding increased responsibility following upgrading.

- There is an overlap between bands which allows very experienced or capable people in one grade to advance to a higher level of pay than relatively inexperienced individuals in the next higher grade.
- The mid-point of the range is taken as the target or market rate applicable to a fully capable individual in a particular job.

Designing a graded salary structure

To design a graded salary structure it is necessary to:

1. Obtain salary survey data on market rates.
2. Carry out a job evaluation exercise which ranks single jobs or groups of comparable jobs in order of importance.
3. Decide on the upper and lower limits of the structure as determined by the highest and lowest paid jobs.
4. Determine the major parameters of the structure, eg a range width of 50 per cent, a differential between grade mid-points of 20 per cent, an overlap between grades of 50 per cent.
5. By reference to the upper and lower limits and the design parameters, work out how many grades are required.
6. Slot the jobs into grades by reference to the job evaluation findings and market rates. Some judgement is required when grouping jobs into grades, and in a competitive situation it may be that market forces have to prevail. Jobs which have to be placed in a higher grade than equity considerations would indicate as appropriate, should be earmarked as special market rate cases (sometimes called red-starring). You may have to recognize that if there is a whole hierarchy of jobs in one occupation category, such as computer staff, where market rate factors are particularly strong, you may need to create a separate market group salary structure for them.

Salary progression

Within a graded salary structure, salaries progress from the starting point (somewhere between the bottom and middle of the range, depending on experience) to the upper limit by means of increments. In the public sector and many large organizations fixed incremental scales are used, where progression depends on service, although an increment may be denied or reduced for a poor performer, or there may be a merit bar. Such incremental scales are easy to manage and fair, in the sense that the rate of advance cannot depend on the subjective judgements or favouritism of the individual's manager, but they do not provide any real scope for rewarding people differentially according to their performance. They are also inflexible and commit the company to expenditure which it may not be able to afford.

179

It is sometimes claimed that these schemes are self-financing because of the process of attrition. The theory is that, in a graded salary structure, when people leave or are promoted from the top of a grade they will be replaced by people with lower salaries at the bottom of the grade. The saving that results from this replacement is said to cover the cost of the fixed incremental scheme. In theory, this can be the case, if staff are evenly spread at each incremental point throughout the grade and if there is a steady flow of leavers from the top of the grade and of entrants at the bottom; but this ideal state seldom, if ever, exists. There may be some savings, but in a typical scheme with increments amounting to 5 per cent of salary, the increase to the payroll costs is still likely to be between 3 and 4 per cent.

The problem is to decide on a fair way of relating reward to performance within an incremental system. A performance appraisal system which is based on objective judgements, as described in Chapter 10, helps. Many companies adopt a policy of allowing a percentage of payroll costs for merit – say 5 per cent – and allowing managers to allocate more or less than the 5 per cent to above or below average performers as assessed in the performance review. The control is that the total payroll increase should not exceed the allowance of, in this example, 5 per cent. It is advisable to exercise a further check on the distribution of awards to ensure that it is not unduly eccentric. Some managers have been known to want to give a few stars excessive increases, which means neglecting the good average performer, who needs to be encouraged as well as the superman or woman.

Other companies, who are wedded to fixed incremental systems, either because they are convenient or because trade unions like them, cater for specially meritorious staff by awarding bonuses. Typical bonus payments in these companies range from between 5 and 10 per cent of salary. Bonuses of this kind are useful to reward people at the top of their salary scale, who are still doing particularly well but cannot be promoted.

It is, of course, also possible in some jobs to relate rewards more directly to performance; the use of bonus schemes is discussed later in this chapter.

Wage structures

The typical wage structure consists of rates for each job which, if there is a trade union, will be fixed by negotiation. The jobs may be graded as skilled, semi-skilled or unskilled and there may be agreed premium payments for possessing special skills, operating certain machines or equipment, or working in dangerous or unpleasant conditions.

It is possible to have a system of merit rating which allows for merit payments on top of the flat day rate, but trade unions are not usually in favour of such payments.

Some companies successfully operate flat day rate systems without any extra payments for output or effort, although they will probably be forced to pay above the going rate. Many firms, however, have some form of payment by results scheme; the use of such systems is discussed in the next section.

PAYMENT BY RESULTS AND BONUS SCHEMES

The principle of relating rewards to performance or effort is a sound one. The problem is to introduce and maintain an effective system. When considering a scheme you need to be aware of:

- The criteria for success.
- The application of payment by results schemes.
- The use of bonus and commission schemes and incentives for managers and other staff.
- The role of profit sharing.

Criteria for success

Bonus schemes often fail to achieve their objective of encouraging better performance. They will not succeed unless they satisfy the following criteria:

1. The amount paid should be significant. There is no point in having a scheme directly related to performance which does not provide a reasonable opportunity to earn at least 10 per cent of base salary, and preferably 20 to 30 per cent.
2. The scheme should be sensitive enough to ensure that rewards are proportionate to achievements.
3. There should be as direct a link as possible between the effort or contribution and the reward.
4. The scheme should be easy to comprehend.
5. The scheme should be seen to be fair.
6. There should not be an undue delay between the effort and the reward.
7. Adequate provision must be made for revising the scheme in changing circumstances.
8. An upper limit should be defined on earnings from the scheme to prevent it getting out of hand. The upper limit will depend on the nature of the scheme, but there are few schemes where it can justifiably exceed 50 per cent.

9. The scheme must be managed effectively. It must not be allowed to 'drift', which means letting the rates go slack so that earnings can increase without a proportionate increase in performance.
10. The scheme should benefit not only the individual but also the company. It should not be too costly to run.

Payment by results schemes

Payment by results schemes usually pay either piece rates – so much per unit – or are based on time allowed. In the latter system, a worker is paid his basic bonus rate if he completes the job in the time allowed (which should have been determined by work study); but if he completes the job in less time he gains the advantage of the time saved, as he is still paid for the original time allowed. Thus, an operator who completes a job timed at 60 hours in 40 hours would receive a bonus of 50 per cent of his bonus rate, ie $((60-40)/40 \times 100$.

Schemes can be applied to individual workers where they operate in isolation from their colleagues, or to groups of workers whose output is interdependent. A group scheme has the advantages of encouraging team spirit, breaking down demarcation lines and encouraging the group to discipline itself to achieve targets.

Piece work or time allowed systems have often been criticized because it is difficult to prevent wage drift. However hard it tries, management comes up against strong opposition if it wants to tighten rates. A negotiated bonus scheme will allow the firm to alter rates in consultation with the union, but often stipulates that this can only take place when there has been a change of method, a change in the product or a mistake in the original calculation. But drift can occur because operators cut corners during the work or because supervisors or rate fixers too easily allow rates to be revised upwards under pressure from the union. However, if the scheme is based on proper work study and if standards are monitored continuously and can be altered if they are no longer appropriate, then payment by results schemes can benefit both the workers and the company.

Measured day work

In situations where it is not possible to meet all the criteria for a successful payment by results scheme some companies, rather than revert to ordinary day work, introduce what is called measured day work. In this arrangement the pay of the employee is fixed, on the understanding that he will maintain a specified level of performance as defined by work study. In the shorter term he is guaranteed his bonus on the understanding that he will meet the defined performance levels. If he fails to do so over the longer term, the standard and the bonus level are reduced.

The advantages of measured day work are that a steady and more easily managed base is provided, standards can be set which are not subject to constant change and wage drift can therefore be more easily controlled. Such schemes, however, are only workable in process or assembly line operations where the job cycle is long, and they depend on meticulous work study.

Bonuses

Bonuses are additions to basic salary in the form of a lump sum which is related in some defined way to performance. Their principal aim is to provide an incentive and a reward for exceptional effort.

Perhaps the most important use of bonuses is in a highly entrepreneurial environment, particularly for chief executives and senior marketing and sales executives.

The criteria which bonus schemes should satisfy are essentially the same as for any incentive scheme. It is particularly important, however, to ensure that:

- After-tax awards should be high enough to encourage acceptance of high and exacting performance standards. The proportion of basic salary which should be achievable if reasonably demanding targets are achieved should be at least 20 to 30 per cent and could be as high as 40 to 50 per cent.
- The factors influencing the size of bonus should be quantifiable and the individual should have a substantial amount of control over them.
- The scheme should be revisable at predetermined intervals and an upper limit of bonus earnings should be set.

In a bonus fund scheme, a bonus fund is derived from a proportion of profits achieved above a predetermined figure. This is then distributed to individuals in proportion to their salaries. Individual bonus schemes can be related to predetermined company profit targets or targets in areas such as sales or manufacturing over which the executive has substantial control.

Incentive schemes for sales staff

The main types of cash-based incentive schemes are either basic salary and commission on sales volume, or basic salary and commission on the contribution to profits and fixed costs of the sales of each product or group of products. As in any other form of incentive scheme, the reward must be fair in relation to effort and, particularly for sales staff, it should be based on attainable and agreed targets that can be adjusted if factors outside personal control affect the sales achieved. The target bonus level is typically of the order of 33 per cent of base salary.

Profit sharing schemes

Profit sharing schemes provide for the employer to pay special sums in the form of cash or shares, the amount of which is related to the profits of the business. The main objectives of profit sharing are as follows:

- To encourage employees to identify themselves more closely with the company by developing common concern for its progress.
- To stimulate greater interest in and understanding of the business and its operating environment among employees.
- To encourage better co-operation between management and employees.
- To recognize that employees have a moral right to share in the profits they have helped to produce.
- To demonstrate in practical terms the goodwill of the company towards its employees.

Note that none of these objectives mentions a direct impact on productivity or profits. Profit sharing does not and cannot provide individual incentive because there is no clear relationship with individual effort. The payment does not follow immediately after the effort and does not therefore reinforce performance. Also, the methods of calculation may often be complex and need full and careful explanation to ensure that employees understand how their annual share is determined. However, to meet one of the most important objectives of human resource management, ie increasing identification and achieving a sense of common purpose, profit sharing can play an important role.

Employee shareholding

The principal benefit of shareholding over cash profit sharing is the sense of ownership it provides and the effect this is likely to have in terms of a long-term change of attitude. The major problems are: first, that the company's share price may fluctuate for external reasons unconnected with company performance and second, the moral dilemma of tying up people's savings with their employer. Many employees would still prefer cash at the time the profit is made, to tax-protected shares on a deferred basis. Much will also depend on union attitudes and the encouragement members are given to accept company proposals.

Shares can be issued as an alternative to cash in a profit sharing scheme. In public companies, share issues must be approved by shareholders.

Share options and share savings schemes

Share options are based on options granted, usually without payment, to employees to purchase shares in the company at present market value. The option may be exercised for a period of years, during which time the employee exercises it when the shares stand at a higher value. The gain made from this form of acquisition and sale is of course subject to tax, but in the UK concessions are available under current financial legislation. Conditions covering these options are complex, and specialist advice should be sought in planning the detailed provisions of such a scheme.

Share savings schemes in the UK are based on save-as-you-earn contracts between employers and employees, with the purpose of share option purchase.

EMPLOYEE BENEFITS

Employee benefits are items in the total package offered to employees over and above salary, which increase their wealth or well-being at some cost to the employer. They are also commonly called fringe benefits, perquisites or 'perks' and non-wage benefits. None of these terms conveys the fact that benefits can frequently add up to around one-third of payroll costs; they are no longer merely the icing on the cake of cash remuneration, but a considerable part of it. Items such as pensions, sick pay, holidays and a varying range of other benefits are an integral part of every company's conditions of employment.

The last 20 years have seen an unprecedented growth in the range of benefits provided. Some of this growth has been hasty and ill considered: a short-term response to pressures imposed by the actual or supposed effects of taxation and by the well-publicized activities of the more cavalier elements in the salary market. A mythology has grown up about the existence of all kinds of extraordinary benefits, especially at top management level, which does not reflect practice in the vast majority of companies.

Benefits fall into the following five categories:

1. Pension schemes.
2. Other provisions for personal security and financial protection, ie insurances, sick pay, redundancy cover and special service contracts.

3. Entitlements recognizing the interface between work and domestic needs or responsibilities, ie holidays and other forms of leave, early or phased retirement options and preparation for retirement provisions.
4. Additional financial assistance, ie loans, house purchase assistance, relocation assistance, credit cards, discounts, fees to professional bodies etc.
5. Other benefits, ie cars, subsidized meals and 'fringe' items which improve employees' standard of living.

A detailed discussion of these benefits is outside the scope of this book. All that need be said at this stage is that whatever else happens, your range of benefits must be competitive with what is supplied for comparable jobs elsewhere. This is particularly the case with pension schemes, holidays, sickness benefits and, at executive level, company cars. For further information on employee benefits see the 'Employee Benefits' chapter in *A Handbook of Salary Administration* by Michael Armstrong and Helen Murlis (Kogan Page, 1987).

PAY ADMINISTRATION

You need to establish and maintain procedures which will ensure that pay policies are implemented and pay budgets are controlled. The areas where such procedures are required are as follows:

- Obtaining information on market rates.
- Grading or regrading jobs by means of job evaluation.
- Fixing or amending rates of pay for jobs.
- Fixing rates of pay for new starters and following promotion or an increase in responsibility.
- Conducting general reviews of levels of pay.
- Awarding merit increases and other performance- or service-related pay increments.
- Administering and maintaining bonus, incentive and profit sharing schemes.
- Fixing additional rates to be paid for particular responsibilities or special working conditions.
- Administering and reviewing the employee benefit system.
- Setting, monitoring and controlling pay budgets.

12. Occupational Health and Safety

A human resource management programme has to include systems which take care of the health and safety at work of employees. The occupational health and safety programme should be based on the following principles:

1. Industrial disease and accidents result from a multiplicity of factors, but these have to be traced to their root causes, which are usually faults in the management system arising from poor leadership from the top, inadequate supervision, insufficient attention to the design of health and safety into the system, an unsystematic approach to the identification, analysis and elimination of hazards, and poor education and training facilities.
2. The most important function of health and safety programmes is to identify potential hazards, provide effective safety facilities and equipment, and take prompt remedial action. This is only possible if there are:
   - comprehensive and effective systems for reporting all accidents causing damage or injury;
   - adequate accident records and statistics;
   - systematic procedures for carrying out safety checks, inspections and investigations;
   - methods of ensuring that safety equipment is maintained and used;
   - proper means available for persuading managers, supervisors and the work force to pay more attention to health and safety matters.
3. The health and safety policies of the organization should be determined by top management, who must be continuously involved in monitoring health and safety performance and in ensuring that corrective action is taken when necessary.
4. Management and supervisors must be made fully accountable for

187

health and safety performance in the working areas they control.

5. All employees should be given thorough training in safe methods of work and should receive continuing education and guidance on eliminating health and safety hazards and on the prevention of accidents.

To put these principles to work it is necessary to:

- Issue a health and safety statement.
- Introduce an occupational health programme.
- Introduce an accident prevention system.

THE HEALTH AND SAFETY POLICY STATEMENT

The policy statement should be a declaration of the intention of the employer to safeguard the health and safety of his employees. It should emphasize four fundamental points: first, that the safety of employees and the public is of paramount importance; second, that safety will take precedence over expediency; third, that every effort will be made to involve all managers, supervisors and employees in the development and implementation of health and safety procedures; and fourth, that health and safety legislation will be complied with in the spirit as well as the letter of the law.

OCCUPATIONAL HEALTH PROGRAMMES

Occupational health programmes are concerned with the identification and control of health hazards arising from toxic substances, radiation, noise, fatigue and the stresses imposed upon body and mind at work.

Basic approach

In each of these areas the same basic approach is necessary. The first stage is to identify the substances, conditions or processes which are actually or potentially dangerous. The second stage is to evaluate how the hazard arises by studying the nature of the substance or condition and the circumstances in which the danger occurs. This means establishing the point at which a substance or an environmental condition is in danger of becoming harmful, in terms of the intensity and duration of the exposure. It also means that the effect of working methods and processes on the human body and mind has to be examined.

Industrial hygiene research into these matters should be carried out by specialist medical advisers working closely with process engineers and chemists. In particularly hazardous environments, research and advice may be required from members of the growing profession of occupational hygienists.

The final stage is to develop methods of minimizing the risk by exercising control over the use of dangerous substances or over the environment in which the hazard occurs. Control of occupational health and hygiene problems can be achieved by:

- Eliminating the hazard at the source by means of design and process engineering which may, for example, ensure that harmful concentrations of toxic substances are not allowed to contaminate the worker.
- Isolating hazardous operations or substances so that workers do not come into contact with them.
- Changing the process, methods of work or substances used to promote better protection or to remove the risk.
- Providing protective equipment, but only if changes to the design, process or specification cannot completely remove the hazard.
- Training workers to avoid risk by eliminating dangerous or risky practices or by using the protective equipment provided.
- Maintaining plant and equipment to minimize the possibility of harmful emissions.
- Good housekeeping to keep premises and machinery clean and free from toxic substances.
- Regular inspections to ensure that potential health risks are identified in good time.
- Pre-employment medical examinations and regular checks on those exposed to risk.

ACCIDENT PREVENTION

The first step to take in preventing accidents is to identify the actual or potential causes. You can then take a number of preventive actions as described later.

Identifying the causes of accidents

The process of identifying causes is mainly one of conducting inspections, checks and investigations. Some consideration should be given, however, to the general factors that induce accidents, as these will indicate the approach that should be used at the design and inspection stages.

Fundamentally it is the system of work to which human beings are exposed that is the cause of accidents. Carelessness, fatigue, lack of knowledge, inexperience, inadequate training or poor supervision may, in different degrees, be the immediate causes, but all these factors are related to the basic system of work.

The causes of accidents can therefore be divided into two main areas:

1. Those related to the system of work, which are the basic reasons for most accidents.
2. Those related to personal factors, which in many cases arise from the system of work, but which might not have happened if there had been no human failure at or near the point of time when the accident occurred.

System of work factors

The main factors in the system of work which induce accidents are:

- Unsafely designed machinery, plant and processes.
- Congested layouts.
- Unguarded or inadequately guarded machinery.
- Defective plant, materials or working conditions; rough, sharp, or obstructive objects; slippery or greasy conditions; decayed, corroded, frayed or cracked containers, wires, conveyor belts or piping; badly maintained machinery.
- Poor housekeeping – congestion, blocked gangways or exits; inadequate disposal arrangements for swarf or other waste products; lack of storage facilities; unclean working conditions.
- Inadequate lighting, glare.
- Inadequate ventilation or systems for removing toxic fumes from the working environment.
- Lack of protective clothing or devices.

It should be noted that although these factors are all connected with the system of work they all result from a human failure at some time.

Personal factors

The personal factors causing accidents are:

- Using equipment unsafely – deliberately or through fatigue.
- Unsafe loading and placing of materials or parts on machines or transport systems.
- Operating without sufficient clearance.
- Operating at an unsafe speed.
- Making safety devices inoperative to reduce interference and speed up work.

- Distractions from other people, noise or events taking place in the workshop.
- Failure to use protective clothing or devices.

Any of these factors may result from personal failures such as carelessness, recklessness, laziness, impatience, lack of consideration; or inadequate knowledge, training, skill or supervision.

Preventive actions

The preventive actions you should take are:

- Take account of safety factors at the design stage – building safety into the system.
- Design safety equipment and protective devices and provide protective clothing.
- Carry out regular inspections and checks and take action to eliminate risks.
- Investigate all incidents resulting in damage to establish the cause and to initiate corrective action.
- Develop an effective health and safety organization.
- Maintain good records and statistics which will identify problem areas and unsatisfactory trends.
- Conduct a continuous programme of education and training on safe working habits and methods of avoiding accidents.

PART IV

Human Resource Development

Introduction

The process of human resource development starts from the strategic plans of the enterprise which define where the business is going and, broadly, the resources required to get there. These strategies are translated by human resource planning into more specific definitions of how many and what sort of people will be needed in the future. Human resource development takes these plans and the raw material provided by recruitment and basic training, and transforms them by means of development programmes to meet the present and future requirements of the organisation.

13. Training and Developing People

AIMS

Human resource development (HRD) programmes help to ensure that the organization has the people with the skills and knowledge it needs to achieve its strategic objectives. They aim to train new employees to the level of performance required in their jobs quickly and economically and to develop the abilities of existing staff so that performance in their present jobs is improved and they are prepared to take on increased responsibilities in the future.

Approaches

The approaches used by HRD in achieving these aims have been defined as follows:

The identification of needed skills and active management of employee learning for the long-range future in relation to explicit corporate and business strategies. (Douglas Hall)

Those learning experiences which are organized, for a specified time, and designed to bring about the possibility of behavioural change. (Leonard Nadler)

Basis

The starting point of the HRD programme is the strategic plan of the enterprise which is translated into human resource plans, as described in Chapter 8. These plans define requirements in numerical terms and also indicate the new or additional skills and expertise the organization requires because of product or market development plans, or technological change. A further important source of information for HRD will be the output of appraisal procedures, as described in Chapter 10, which identifies individual and corporate training and development needs.

ACTIVITIES

Human resource development is about two things: training and development.

Training

Training fills the gap between what someone can do and what he should be able to do. Its first aim is to ensure that, as quickly as possible, people can reach an acceptable level in their jobs. Training then builds on this foundation by enhancing skills and knowledge as required to improve performance in the present job or to develop potential for the future.

Development

Development can be defined as the modification of behaviour through experience. It provides for people to do better in existing jobs and prepares them for greater responsibility in the future. It builds on strengths and helps to overcome weaknesses, and ensures that the organization has the expertise it needs.

Development operates at all levels. For shop floor and more junior supervisory, office, technical and professional staff it should be programmed to provide the right training at the right time and to broaden people's expertise and abilities by giving them new tasks to carry out. Performance appraisal and coaching play an important part.

At a higher level, management development programmes, as described later in this chapter, aim systematically to identify talent, improve skills, widen experience and help people to grow in their ability to accept greater responsibility.

THE PAY-OFFS

The pay-offs you can get from systematically training and developing your staff are that you will:

- Provide the organization with the skills and expertise it needs to achieve its strategic objectives.
- Shorten learning time, so that new recruits reach the performance level of the fully experienced and effective worker as quickly and economically as possible.
- Improve the efficiency and effectiveness of existing employees.
- Help people to develop their natural abilities, so that your company

can meet its future human resource requirements in terms both of quality and quantity from within the organization.

You should regard your HRD programme as an investment. You have to spend money on it, but if properly spent, that money will give you a worthwhile return.

WHAT YOU NEED TO KNOW AND DO

To introduce and maintain an effective HRD programme you need to:

1. Understand the basic principles of how people learn – this will provide you with the knowledge of how to plan and deliver training programmes.
2. Appreciate the concept of systematic training – what you have to do to get results.
3. Know how to identify training and development needs.
4. Be able to plan training and development programmes which will satisfy identified needs. These will include formal and informal and on- or off-the-job courses.
5. Know how to select and use appropriate training techniques.
6. Understand how to get the best out of management development programmes.
7. Take steps to evaluate the results of training and development programmes and use the results of such evaluations to improve their effectiveness.

How people learn

Training works best if it is based on an appreciation of how people learn. The ten conditions required for successful learning are:

1. The individual must be motivated to learn – and he will be motivated if he thinks there is something in it for him.
2. The learner should gain satisfaction from learning.
3. Standards of performance and targets to be attained should be set for the learner.
4. The learner needs guidance in the shape of a sense of direction and 'feedback' on how he is doing.
5. Learning is an active not a passive process. People learn best by doing and getting involved, not just by listening.
6. Training techniques should be used with discrimination to fit the objectives of the training programme and the needs of the individual.

7. Learning methods should be varied to maintain interest.
8. Time should be allowed to absorb the learning. The existence of the 'learning curve', which represents the time taken to acquire skills, should always be remembered when planning courses and reviewing progress.
9. The learner needs reinforcement of correct behaviour. In other words, he needs to know when he is doing well to ensure that he retains good habits and skills and is encouraged to learn more.
10. As a process, learning can operate at a number of different levels of complexity, depending on the job. Training programmes and techniques need to be adjusted accordingly.

Systematic training

To be successful, you need to adopt a systematic approach to training, and this means:

- Identifying and analysing training needs.
- Defining training objectives – training must aim to achieve measurable goals expressed in terms of improvements and changes in behaviour which lead to better performance.
- Preparing training plans which will meet objectives – these will describe the costs and benefits of the proposed training programmes.
- Implementing training plans.
- Monitoring and analysing results.
- Feeding back the results of evaluation so that training can be improved.

Identifying training needs

Training must be relevant. Too often it is not. It happens because someone has heard that it is a good thing: 'Let's have a course for trainees', 'Let's run a supervisory training programme', 'Let's send Smith on this course described in the leaflet I got this morning'. The content of these *ad hoc* courses may have little or nothing to do with what the trainees really need to learn. Learning objectives are not set, inappropriate methods are used, the trainee finds it difficult to relate what he has learnt in the classroom or training workshop to what he actually has to do, and it is next to impossible to evaluate results.

One of the biggest problems you will meet in off-the-job training is that of transferring what is learnt on the course to the work place. This problem can be solved if the training course is based on an analysis of what people have to do and need to know. Even when training is on-the-job, it will be much better if it is based on an analysis of training needs, so that skills can be taught and experience can be planned in a way which will satisfy those needs.

Methods of identification I: job and skills analysis
The identification of training needs starts, as do so many other aspects of managing human resources, from job analysis, which describes the tasks that are carried out. From this is derived the training specification, which sets out the characteristics that the worker should have in order to perform these tasks successfully. The characteristics are:

- *Knowledge*: what the worker needs to know. It may be professional, technical or commercial knowledge. It may be about the machines or equipment to be operated, the products to be sold, the customers to be dealt with, or the problems that will be encountered and how they should be dealt with.
- *Skills*: what the worker needs to be able to do if results are to be achieved and knowledge is to be used properly. Skills may be manual, intellectual, mental, perceptual or social.
- *Attitudes*: the disposition to behave or to perform in a way which is in accordance with the requirements of the work.

Task analysis techniques define for each task:

- Its relative significance to the successful performance of the job as a whole.
- The level of skill or knowledge required to perform it.
- The typical faults that can occur, how they should be recognized, what causes them and what can be done to avoid or remedy them.
- The instructional techniques and the type and length of experience required to become proficient in each task.

Methods of identification II: performance analysis
Although the starting point for identifying training needs is job analysis, you have to go beyond this in assessing the training needs of experienced workers. This further analysis studies what individuals or groups of workers are actually achieving against what they are expected to do.

The information you need is obtained from the process of performance appraisal described in Chapter 10. A results-oriented approach compares achievements with agreed targets or standards of performance for each task. If results are not up to standard, the manager and subordinate jointly assess why this has happened. It may be for reasons beyond the employee's control, but if it is attributable to him in any way, the reasons

201

for things going wrong are discussed and agreement reached on what should be done about them. The action may be mainly up to the employee, but if he requires and deserves help, guidance or further instruction then this should be provided by the boss through coaching or, on the boss's recommendation, by the company through training courses or secondments to gain experience.

A performance appraisal system should identify individual training needs. If the results of the whole scheme are analysed, information should be obtained on collective training needs which would be satisfied by company courses.

In addition to analysing the results of performance appraisal, you should continually be on the alert for other evidence of weaknesses in individuals or those common to a number of people. For example, if the quality of written reports is generally low, a report writing course could be laid on.

Planning training courses

You should never plan a training course without having first clarified training needs. You must then set training or learning objectives. These are best expressed in the form of a statement of what you would expect the trainee to know and be able to do if he satisfactorily completed the course. The statement should start with the words: 'On completing this course the trainee will be able to...'.

Having set objectives, you can then decide on:

1. *The content of the course*, as established by job and task analysis and information from performance appraisals.
2. *Training techniques*, as described in the next section.
3. *The location*, which can either be:
   - off-the-job, where the advantages are that training can be concentrated, planned, without distractions, and given by qualified trainers. There are, however, disadvantages, including the problems referred to earlier of transferring knowledge and skills from what is sometimes called 'the learning situation' to the place of work, and the danger of training becoming irrelevant because it is divorced from reality;
   - on-the-job, where the advantages are that it should be practical and immediately relevant; but the disadvantages are that the quality of instruction may be poor, the training programme may not have been properly planned, and the trainee is unable to concentrate on learning, especially those aspects dealing with knowledge and skills.

As a generalization, training off-the-job is best for imparting knowledge and basic skills, especially manual skills. Training on-the-job is best for developing basic skills and the application of knowledge, but it must be planned and given by managers and supervisors who have themselves been trained in how to instruct. Many training programmes are composed of a judicious mix of off- and on-the-job training.

4. *The duration of training*, which obviously depends upon how much learning has to take place. An apprenticeship might involve a prolonged course mixing theoretical, practical, on- and off-the-job training. Or the training could comprise a short sharp two- or three-day course to teach non-financial managers how to understand accounts, or a carefully sequenced programme of experience, or a mix of planned experienced, short internal courses and longer external courses, designed as part of a management development programme.

5. *Responsibility for training*: it is essential to put someone in charge – a professional training officer if the length and depth of the course requires it, or a designated manager who is given the task as part of his other responsibilities. Full- or part-time lecturers or instructors have to be nominated and, if they are from within the company, they must be trained in the skills they have to use.

6. *Evaluation*: the methods used to assess the results of training. These start from the definition of training objectives and then attempt to measure how far these objectives have been achieved. Where training is concerned with manual or other basic skills its effectiveness can be measured first by classroom tests, followed up by analysis of the extent to which these skills have been applied successfully at work.

Supervisory and management training may be more difficult to evaluate because it is not always easy to measure the effect of what has been learned. There are a number of levels at which such training can be evaluated, which become progressively harder to assess, namely:

- reactions from course members as to whether they feel that the course has achieved its objectives;
- reports from course members and their managers on the changes that have been introduced or the improvements in the performance of individuals following the training;
- the impact of training on the results achieved by the department;
- the impact of training on the results achieved by the company.

Training techniques

The training techniques you use should be related to the situation in which training is being given and the type of training needs you aim to satisfy. The factors that affect how people learn, as described earlier in this chapter, are also important, especially the needs to motivate, to set standards, to make learning an active process, to allow time to absorb the learning and to give the learner reinforcement of correct behaviour. The main training techniques available are summarized below.

Job instruction
Job instruction techniques are based on skills analysis. The sequence of instruction should follow three stages:

1. *Preparation*: the instructor has a plan for presenting the subject matter and for using appropriate teaching methods and aids.
2. *Presentation*: this should consist of a combination of telling and showing (demonstration). People will not learn much by simply using their ears. They need to observe with their eyes what happens as well.
3. *Practice*: the learner imitates the instructor and repeats the operation under guidance. The aims are to reach the target level of performance for each element of the total task and to achieve the smooth combination of these elements into a whole job pattern.

The job instruction sequence therefore combines the three processes of hearing, seeing and doing. The last is the most important, because learning is essentially an active process. Reinforcement in the shape of practice and feedback sessions should be built into the programme and the more the trainee can measure his own performance and assess his own progress, the better.

Coaching
Instruction is a planned and formalized procedure which most often takes place off-the-job. In contrast, coaching is more informal and always happens on-the-job. It takes the form of an interaction between the boss and his subordinate whenever it is believed that the latter will benefit from guidance.

It could be said that every time you ask a subordinate to do anything and tell him how to do it or, preferably, get him to tell you how he proposes to do it, then you are in a coaching situation. The same applies every time you discuss the outcome of a task and ask your subordinate to tell you about it. In both cases, you have the opportunity to provide guidance on how to carry out a new task or how to improve performance on an existing one.

A slightly more formal approach to coaching is initiated by the appraisal interview in a results-oriented scheme as described in Chapter 10. This can produce an analysis of areas for improvement and an agreement on the help the manager will provide to his subordinate by a programme of coaching.

Coaching is most effective if it takes place as part of the normal process of management. This type of coaching is carried out by:

- Making a subordinate aware of how he is managing by, for example, asking questions on how well he has thought through what he is doing.
- Controlled delegation, ie taking care that, when giving a subordinate a task, he knows how to do it or where he can get help.
- Using any working situations which arise as teaching opportunities.
- Setting individual projects and assignments and, without breathing too closely down the individual's neck, monitoring how he is getting on.
- Spending time in looking at higher level problems as well as discussing the immediate job (this is an important technique for developing people's potential).

Lecturing

A lecture is a classic method of instruction. It may be an efficient way to encapsulate concepts and facts, but it is not always an effective means by itself of getting the message across, especially if it relies mainly upon the spoken word and provides no visual aids to reinforce verbal content.

Many people are bad lecturers because they are boring, disorganized or unaware of the best way to present their topic. No one should ever be asked to speak on a course without first having been trained in how to make presentations, and this training must include plenty of practice sessions.

When lecturing or making presentations, the things to do are:

1. *Prepare thoroughly*: decide what you are trying to achieve, get all the facts relevant to that objective, distil these into no more than three positive messages so that your facts and opinions can be grouped under these headings (no more than three ideas because that is all that most people can absorb at a time).
2. *Structure the talk carefully*: divide it into three parts – an introduction which tells your audience what you are intending to

achieve and the structure of your talk, a middle in which your three messages are presented clearly, and a conclusion which summarizes what they have just heard. In other words, your talk should have a beginning, a middle, and an end. Successively, in each section, you should tell your audience what you are going to say, then say it and then tell them what you have said. Your three messages will thus have been presented three times. This is no bad thing; it is, in fact, the principle of reinforcement in action.

3. *Provide signposts*: keep reminding people of where you have gone to and where you are going – reinforcement again.

4. *Keep it snappy*: the maximum time any talk should ever last is 40 minutes. If you go that far, you need to keep the interest going by the various methods described below.

5. *Start and end with a bang*: get the audience's attention with a positive beginning and send them away feeling inspired and enlightened with a stimulating conclusion.

6. *Get your delivery right*: vary your talk, change pace – not too fast not too slow, although most people talk too quickly out of nervousness. Change the pitch of your voice; try to avoid using a monotonous voice, go up at the end of the sentence rather than down. Use pregnant pauses – the sound of silence – to provide emphasis and a chance for people to absorb what you are telling them. Avoid irritating mannerisms. Stand up and speak out.

7. *Use visual aids*: your audience will probably only absorb about one-third of what you say. Reinforce your message with visual aids. Appeal to more than one sense at a time. Flip charts, slides, overhead projectors and so on all add interest and provide good back up. But don't overdo them, and keep them simple.

8. *Don't read your talk*: there is nothing more boring than a speaker who slavishly follows his text. You don't have to write it all down and read it out if you prepare your notes carefully and rehearse. Even if you stumble now and again for a word, no one will mind. Liveliness, even with the occasional mistake, is preferable to monotony every time.

9. *Prepare your notes*: jot down the headings for each section on postcards, to which you can refer easily. Learn your opening sentence off by heart so that you can get off to a confident start. Do the same at the end. If you are really worried about breaking down, have a full text available for reference. But don't worry; there is no reason why it should happen, especially if you rehearse thoroughly.

10. *Rehearse*: rehearsal is vital. It instils confidence, helps you to get your timing right, enables you to polish your opening and closing

remarks, and ensures that your talk and your visual aids are co-ordinated.

Do-it-yourself training

The principle behind do-it-yourself training is that people will retain more if they find out things for themselves. Do-it-yourself training operates by:

- Starting from a definition of what someone needs to know and do to perform a job.
- Establishing where the information is available.
- Giving the trainee an outline of the information he has to obtain and where and from whom he can get it.
- Briefing the trainee's boss and colleagues on the help they should give him.
- Preparing a timetable for the training programme.
- Arranging for the trainee's progress to be monitored by his boss and/or a training officer.

Action learning

Action learning is a training method, devised by Professor Revons, which helps managers to develop their talents by being exposed to real problems. They are required to analyse them, formulate recommendations and then, instead of being satisfied with a report, take action. This approach accords with the belief that managers learn best by doing rather than by being taught and that all good training should be problem-based and action-oriented.

Participative training exercises

Managers may learn to manage best by managing under a good manager, but there is still scope to acquire fresh insights into the process of management away from work. These insights will be more real if course members can participate in case studies which present them with management problems to solve, or simulations which place them in situations where they have to exercise managerial skills. Managers will learn as much from each other as from their tutor in these situations, because they encourage course members to share their experience.

Computer-based training

Computers can be used to simulate actual situations so that trainees can 'learn by doing'. For example, technicians can be trained in trouble-shooting and repairing electronic circuitry by looking at circuit dia-grams displayed on the screen and using a light pen to measure voltages at different points on the circuit. When faults are diagnosed, 'repairs' are effected by means of the light pen, this time employed as a soldering iron. Computers can also be used to provide a database which trainees can access through a computer terminal.

Video

Video can be used to present material specially prepared for the company in an attractive and compelling way. It can get the training message across effectively in a number of different locations, but there is no scope for interaction.

Interactive video

Interactive video combines the powerful training technology of computer-based learning with the use of video. Interactive video can offer the trainer the best of both worlds. It is individualized, interactive and random-access (like computer-based training), but can also present realistic still and moving visuals with or without sound (like video). As a bonus, most video discs also have features like dual or stereo sound tracks, a wide variety of slow-motion and fast-scan relay speeds, freeze frame and single-step frame, endless repetition of any scene or chapter, and customized keypads for specified applications.

Management development

If you want to ensure that your organization has the effective managers it requires to meet its present and future needs, you should consider introducing a systematic process of management development.

Aims

Management development programmes aim to:

- Improve the performance of managers.
- Identify managers with potential and ensure that they get the necessary training and experience to fit them for greater responsibility.
- Provide, so far as possible, management succession from within the company.

Methods

Your management development strategy should be to provide an environment in which people can grow, you should not attempt to force feed them. The starting point should be to recruit people who are largely self-motivated and will react positively to any opportunities. Then you give them the chance to develop by taking responsibility and learning as they go along. If they are well-motivated they will find out for themselves what they need to know and do – the best form of management development is always self-development.

This does not mean that the company and its managers have not got a role to play. First, the opportunities available and the working environment must be conducive to growth. Second, even self- motivated people need some help and guidance and the provision of opportunities to learn. Third, you have to identify those with potential and monitor their progress to ensure that they are given the scope and assistance they deserve.

Although individual encouragement and guidance should provide the foundation for your management development programme, the following techniques will help you to get the most out of it:

1. *Organization analysis*: reviews present organization weaknesses and identifies future demands on management.
2. *Management review*: analyses existing management resources and future requirements in the light of the organization analysis.
3. *A system of accountable management*: ensures that managers understand what they have to do and achieve and are held accountable for their results. Reviews of results against targets indicate where improvement is required.
4. *Performance appraisal*: linked to a system of accountable management, identifies strengths, weaknesses, potential and training needs.
5. *Management inventory*: the information derived from the first four stages of the management development process should be combined to give you an overall picture of the strengths and weaknesses of your managers. This will form the basis for career planning and management training programmes.

One way of looking at your management is to categorize them along the lines that the Boston Consulting Group has developed for analysing products or businesses. They say that you can place any product in one of the four boxes shown in Figure 13.1. The same approval can be used for your managerial resources, who can be classified in one of four similar boxes as shown in Figure 13.2.

The *rising stars* are people with potential, who will benefit from career planning, wider experience and management training. You may wish to 'fast track' them by rapid promotion or by offering more challenging opportunities. They should be listed and looked after. This may mean paying over the odds to demonstrate that you

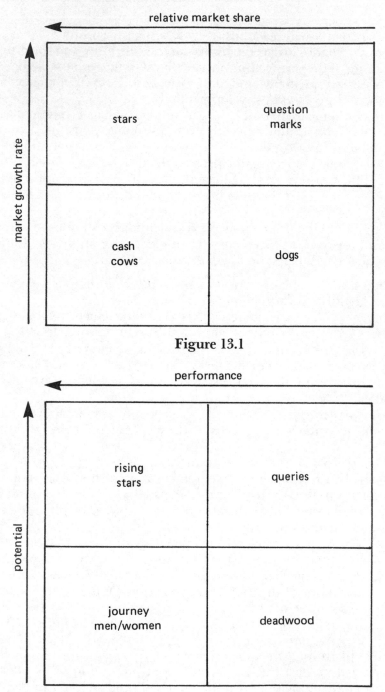

Figure 13.1

Figure 13.2

value them and to keep them from straying further afield. It does not mean setting up a row of crown princes whose future is guaranteed and whose path to the top is made easy. They have to know that they have only been given these opportunities because they have performed well so far, and that the demands made on them in the future are going to be even greater. There is no easy way to the top and they must realize that they will have to work their passage, and that, while you have your eye on them and are going to help their development, in the last analysis it will be up to them.

The *journey men* or *women* are the people on whom you depend to get things done. They are the backbones of the organization. They are sometimes called workhorses, but this is a somewhat derogatory term. They are not necessarily going to rise much above their present level, but they are useful and dependable and they still need training in new techniques and skills. They also need the encouragement and motivation provided by varying their responsibilities, introducing new opportunities wherever this can be arranged, and assuring them that they are doing a worthwhile job.

The *queries* are those managers who for one reason or another do not seem to be making the grade. They may have the ability but not the motivation, or they may have the motivation but not the ability. In the latter case it is worth trying to establish and satisfy training needs. They are clearly worth saving, if that is at all possible. People with ability who lack motivation may present a bigger problem. It might be a good thing to find out why they are not motivated and do something about it if you can (see Chapter 5). You should give them the chance and any help they deserve; but if they don't want to do it, they won't. If all your warnings fail to achieve improvement, the best thing you can do is let them go.

The *deadwood* are the people – one hopes few in number, if they exist at all – who ought to go. As long as all else in the shape of training and encouragement has failed, there is no point in keeping them – for their sake as well as yours. They could do better elsewhere if they can find a nice square hole into which they will fit.

6. *Planned experience* (career development): this equips managers to do their jobs better and fits them for promotion by ensuring that they have the right variety of experience and guidance, in good time, in the course of their careers. The aims are first, to ensure that people of promise are given a sequence of experience which will equip them for whatever level of responsibility they have the ability to reach and second, to see that they get the direction and guidance that even the best-motivated people need to develop their knowledge and skills and their careers.

Career development programmes involve appraisal, coaching and the provision of 'mentors' whose role is to give guidance and help to the people they are responsible for. They provide learning opportunities and hold regular informal coaching sessions in which the lessons from experience are analysed and new directions for the future are worked out. Mentors offer the people with whom they are concerned the opportunity to discuss work and career development problems. Fears about the future can be brought out into the open and resolved. Opportunities for development can be identified and explained. Mentors should not deal with their own staff. They should be appointed to carry out their functions with specified individuals from other parts of the company and they need to be trained in the skills they have to use, especially coaching techniques.

7. *Management training*: training in specific areas or 'broadening' training to expand the horizons of promising managers can be used to supplement – but not replace – planned experience, as long as the courses are timed and designed to meet particular needs. For example, a manager who has specialized in a function such as marketing, but who has potential in general management, will benefit from an extended business school course for senior executives. He will learn about other functions besides his own, including the overall control of a business, but he will also be exposed to intensive teaching and the challenge of pursuing a demanding programme in the company of his peers. He will absorb a lot simply by mixing with people from other environments who are as good as, if not better than, himself.

PART V

Human Resource Relationships

Introduction

Human resource management as sometimes presented appears to ignore the problems of individuals on the assumption that a patronizing involvement with people's personal affairs is inappropriate. HRM also seems to ignore the existence of trade unions. The message is sometimes presented in simplistic terms, that unions are not really necessary if you have a chief executive who can communicate missions, strategies and core values effectively and keep everyone involved.

But managers have to spend a great deal of time dealing with people's problems and, to get the best out of their staff, they should, when necessary, adopt a 'counselling' approach to help individuals overcome work-related difficulties and improve their performance. It also has to be recognized that employees will not necessarily accept the values handed down to them on a plate. They have their own values and their own interests which they feel may conflict with those of the organization and have to be defended.

HRM in the fullest sense, as presented in this book, has therefore to include methods and programmes for handling people individually and collectively.

14. Handling People Individually

Human resource management aims to promote the common interests of employer and employed in the success of the business, but whatever steps you take to achieve this aim, you will find that there are some people whom you cannot fit into your scheme of things. In spite of all your efforts to train and motivate them, they may be incapable of meeting acceptable standards; or, more sadly, you may be forced to accept that in special circumstances the needs of the organization have to override the needs of some individuals in it. New technology, falling order books, or a history of overmanning may mean that you can no longer retain some staff. As the Americans put it, you could find yourself in a 'down-sizing situation'. There will also be some people who cannot or will not fit themselves to the organization's requirements, while others will have real or imaginary grievances.

Overall, you need to adopt problem-solving techniques to handle these matters, especially those involving individuals who are ill-disciplined, who cannot cope with their work, or who have grievances. You then need to understand the particular approaches you can use in dealing with:

- Disciplinary problems.
- Grievances.
- Redundancy.

PROBLEM SOLVING

Solving people's problems requires the following steps:

1. *Define the problem*: establish what is going wrong.
2. *Get the facts*: find out what has happened, is happening or is about to happen. Compare this with what is supposed to happen. If different people are involved, get both sides of the story and, where possible, check with a third party. Obtain written evidence wherever relevant. Do not rely on hearsay. Try to understand the attitudes and

217

motivation of those concerned. Remember that people will see the situation from their point of view and in terms of their own needs, attitudes and feelings.

3. *Analyse the facts*: identify relevant data and establish the cause or causes of the problem. Do not be misled by symptoms. Get to the root of the matter. Dig into what lies behind the problem.

4. *Consider and evaluate possible courses of action*: agree an objective for a solution. Discuss alternative courses of action with whoever is involved and weigh up the pros and cons of each of them.

5. *Decide and implement*: in discussion with the individual and other people concerned, decide which, on balance, is the preferred course of action. Explain the reasons for your final decision. Then implement.

6. *Monitor implementation*: check on how well the decision is being implemented. Obtain the reactions of those affected. Take further corrective action where necessary.

INTERVIEWING AND COUNSELLING

It may seem an open and shut case, but you should still check the situation with the individual to get information on his reactions, opinions and feelings and, where appropriate, to obtain any explanations he may have to offer. At this meeting you can discuss remedial action.

You will need to get at the true facts and to achieve the willing co-operation of the employee in implementing an agreed solution. You will not do this if you adopt an autocratic approach in situations where it is not relevant, that is, where the employee is worth saving with your advice and help. You will get more co-operation and better results in these circumstances if you adopt the following non-directive counselling approach:

1. Listen with intelligence and sympathy. Someone in difficulties cannot fail to benefit if he is allowed to discuss his problem with a sympathetic listener.

2. Get the problem clearly stated and accepted as a problem by the interviewee as well as the interviewer. The interviewee should be helped to define the problem for himself. If he does this he is much more likely to be interested in solving it.

3. When defining the problem and discussing possible solutions a considerable amount of listening and questioning may be necessary before the point becomes clear, especially when strong

emotions are involved – their presence and clarity of expression seldom go together.

4. When trying to get the employee's point of view, it is often helpful to reflect back to him his key statements in your own words. This checks your understanding and tells him that he is getting through.

5. Stay alert and flexible. You should have a broad plan about how you would like to tackle the interview, but be prepared to change direction in the light of new information.

6. Go through the facts of the case, however unpleasant they may be, but refrain from making derogatory comments during the interview.

7. Try not to get drawn into a futile argument about matters of opinion. If there is a difference in views about the facts, simply record it and check later.

8. Observe behaviour as well as words, which can be misleading. Take note of gestures, manner, tone and inflexion, pauses and others ways of responding.

9. Summarize where you have got to from time to time with a crystallizing statement or question such as: 'Am I right in thinking that your problem boils down to this...?' But don't put words in his mouth.

10. Try to get the interviewee to summarize the situation and, in circumstances such as when an improvement in performance is required, suggest a possible solution. Agree with that solution if you possibly can and encourage the individual to plan its implementation.

HANDLING DISCIPLINARY CASES

When you have to deal with misconduct or incapability you should follow certain basic principles of natural justice which, in the UK, have been established by case law. These are:

1. The individual should know the standards of performance he is expected to achieve and the rules to which he is expected to conform.

2. He should be given a clear indication of where he is falling or the rules he has broken.

3. Except in cases of gross misconduct, he should be given an opportunity to improve before disciplinary action is taken.

4. He should know the nature of the accusation against him.

5. He should be given the opportunity to state his case.

6. The disciplinary tribunal should act in good faith.
7. The employee should be allowed to appeal.

Disciplinary procedure

To ensure that these principles are put into practice, you should have a disciplinary procedure consisting of the following stages:

1. *Informal verbal warnings* stating what has gone wrong and what must be done about it. The statement should be as specific as possible and refer to rules that have been broken or to agreed standards that have not been achieved. Factual evidence should be produced wherever possible. A note for file should be made of the warning.
2. *A formal written warning* if performance or behaviour has not improved after the initial warning. Again, this will state specifically the nature of the problem, referring to rules that have been broken or standards not achieved and reminding the employee of previous informal warnings that he has ignored. It will state that disciplinary action may be taken if improvement does not take place. It will also give a timescale within which improvement must happen.
3. *A final written warning* if the formal warning has not produced the desired result within the timescale. This will express grave concern over the continuance of the problem in spite of previous warnings, and will state explicitly the disciplinary action, such as dismissal, that will be taken if the problem is not overcome.

A timescale for improvement is given but, in cases such as absenteeism or lateness, you may find that the employee makes some effort to improve within the time limit, but when the warning is withdrawn, reverts back to his previous behaviour. In these circumstances, do you have to keep on going through the warning cycle time after time? The answer must be no, and the best approach in these cases is to avoid specifying a date when the final warning period ends. Instead, the final warning letter should simply say that performance will be reviewed on a stated date. If it has not improved, disciplinary action is taken. If it has, no action is taken, but the employee is warned that further deterioration will make him liable for disciplinary action, which may well circumvent the normal procedure by going straight back into the final warning stage and reducing the time between the warning and the review date. If it is clear after this that the employee is incapable of sustaining acceptable standards of performance or behaviour, then disciplinary action is taken. The procedure should include provisions for appeal at the final warning stage or against the disciplinary action.

A procedure such as this is fair both to the employee, if there is a good reason for applying it, and to the manager, in that following the procedure will demonstrate that he has acted reasonably.

It is not easy to apply, however, in cases of gradual deterioration where there has been no major lapse which calls for immediate action. There is a tendency for managers not to want to tackle this sort of problem because they cannot be specific enough about what is wrong. The situation drifts along and when, after a number of years, it is decided that action must take place, it is much harder to pin down the problem. Allowing this to happen can be unfair on the employee. He may not be aware that he is failing to meet your required standards. The longer it goes on, the more difficult it will become for him to understand what is wrong and, if action is delayed excessively, he might find it hard to improve or to find another job.

It cannot be emphasized strongly enough that a fair and effective disciplinary procedure must be based on clearly defined and understood standards and rules. The advantage of a system of results-oriented appraisal, as described in Chapter 10, is that targets and standards are agreed and regular performance reviews take place. This sytem is most applicable to managerial, supervisory and clerical staff, but on the shop floor it is still possible to set standards and require supervisors to ensure that employees know the results of the regular reviews that take place of performance against those standards.

Difficulties in applying a disciplinary procedure such as that described above, can also occur when senior managers are involved. If poor results or deteriorating performance lead to a total lack of confidence in the ability of the manager to sustain the standards required of him, it may not be appropriate to go through the whole procedure. If confidence in a manager has been lost after a reasonable period of time and for good reasons it is best to agree to part, although there should still have been discussions of the problem areas, and these should have referred specifically to results achieved compared with expectations.

Gross misconduct

Sadly, there are times when instant dismissal is justified because of gross misconduct. It is, however, essential to define the offences that make someone liable to the sack. Typically, these include theft, fraud, abusive, violent or drunken behaviour at work, and gross violations of anti-discrimination laws. It is advisable to have a cooling-off period in the shape of a suspension immediately after you are aware of the offence, in order to confirm the facts and ensure that instant dismissal is appropriate. The employee must also be allowed to appeal against the decision.

GRIEVANCES

You should have a procedure which gives people the chance to raise their grievances with their immediate manager and gives them the right to appeal to higher levels of authority, up to the chief executive of the organization, if they feel that their case has not been adequately dealt with.

Use the interviewing/counselling procedures described earlier in this chapter when hearing grievances or appeals. The aim should be to get to the root of the matter and, if there is no justification for being aggrieved, let the individual work this out for himself, with prompting from you as necessary.

REDUNDANCY

Redundancy is the saddest and often the most difficult HRM problem you will ever have to deal with. There are four things you can do to make it less painful:

1. *Plan ahead to avoid redundancy*: this means anticipating future reductions in manpower needs and allowing wastage to take effect. You need to forecast the amount by which the labour force has to be reduced and the likely losses through labour turnover. You can freeze recruitment at the right moment to allow the surplus to be absorbed by wastage.
2. *Minimize the impact of redundancy* by using one or more of the following methods:
   - calling in outside work;
   - withdrawing sub-contracted labour;
   - reducing overtime;
   - transferring staff to other departments or locations;
   - work sharing – splitting jobs between people, or two people doing one job on half days or alternate days;
   - dismissing part-timers;
   - short-time working;
   - temporary layoffs.
3. *Voluntary redundancy*: asking for volunteers, with a suitable pay-off, is one way of reducing the number of compulsory redundancies. Unfortunately, the wrong people may go, ie your good workers who are best able to find other work. You may therefore find yourself going into reverse and having to offer them a special loyalty bonus if they agree to stay on.
4. *Redundancy procedures* should have three aims:
   - to treat employees fairly;

- to reduce suffering as much as possible;
- to protect your own ability to run your business effectively.

These aims are not always compatible. You will want to retain your key workers. Trade unions, on the other hand, will want to adopt the principle of last in, first out, irrespective of the value of each employee to the company.

A formal procedure may not be necessary in a very small concern, but whenever you have a larger number to contend with or are dealing with trade unions, it is as well to have a standard method of dealing with the problem. The points you should include are:

- early warning and consultation with unions and staff;
- the means to be adopted to avoid or reduce redundancies, eg cutting back overtime and the use of temporary staff, short-time working, transfer to other jobs with an appropriate trial period;
- the basis of selection for redundancy. You may start with the principle of last in, first out, but you have to reserve the right to deviate from this principle where selection on the basis of service would prejudice operational efficiency;
- the basis of compensating for redundancy, ie payments made by the company which are additional to the statutory minimum;
- the help the company will give to redundant employees to find other work.

15. Handling People Collectively

Human resource management aims to increase the overall effectiveness of the organization by encouraging the participation and involvement of its members. Commitment to what the organization wants to do is all-important, but it is not inevitable. Individuals and groups of people will not necessarily feel that they are going to be better off it they help the organization. In fact, they will often feel that their own needs and those of the organization conflict. However dedicated the chief executive is to ensuring that his vision will materialize, it will not do so unless he exercises leadership and gets his message across to groups of employees as well as to individuals.

There *are* two sides in most organizations – management and workers. There is a gap, and means have to be found to bridge that gap. Because employees feel that as individuals they will not have the power to protect their interests in this bridge-building exercise, they get together in trade unions or staff associations with whom management has to deal.

Whether or not unions exist, however, it is highly desirable for management to develop other methods of dealing with employees collectively, in order to get them involved through various forms of participation. Sadly, relationships with unions often involve confrontations. Other means must therefore be found of encouraging mutuality – working together in the interests of all.

Handling people collectively means dealing with trade unions or staff associations, if you have them. If you don't, you should have a strategy on how to handle employee relations on a non-union basis, which will include either what you do to keep unions out – if that is what you want – or what you do to establish good relationships with any union you get from the word go. Unions have to be managed like everything else in an organization. Management normally gets the unions it deserves. If it handles them badly – too tough or too weak – the results for the organization can be disastrous.

Your approach to collective dealings should be based on an understanding of:

1. The strategy you want to adopt about union recognition.
2. The respective roles of management and trade unions.
3. The type of procedures you can adopt to regularize relationships with trade unions.
4. The basic techniques of negotiating with unions.
5. How to get involvement through participation, which will include traditional forms of joint consultation as well as the more recent Japanese import of quality circles.

RECOGNITION STRATEGY

If you do not have trade unions you will have to decide, in the event of a demand for representation or an approach from a union, whether or not you want to keep them out by whatever means are available. Alternatively, you will have to consider if you are gracefully prepared to accept the inevitable, with the proviso that you want the most appropriate union you can get and an agreement which protects your rights as an employer as well as the rights of the employees the union represents.

Keeping unions out

If you are unhappy about trade unions, these are the positive steps you can take to help your staff feel that they do not need to be represented:

1. Demonstrate by the way you treat and pay them that they have nothing to gain from joining a union.
2. Set up procedures that will prove to your employees that you are prepared to treat them fairly. The most important procedure will deal with grievances (see Chapter 14), but you should consider developing and publishing policies on such matters as remuneration, equal opportunities, the introduction of new technology, redundancy, training, health and safety, participation and welfare.
3. Set up formal joint consultation procedures to deal with the matters referred to above or any other issue which affects employees. Involvement in quality and productivity improvement drives could be a part of this process.

All these positive approaches are desirable, whether or not you are concerned about the encroachment of unions. Some employers go one step further, however, and encourage the formation of staff associations, often with full negotiating rights. It is hoped that these will act as a tame company union and keep undesirable unions at bay. It does not always work: either the staff union becomes just as aggressive as a trade union and has to be bribed with over-generous settlements, or it fails to do its job properly and the door is opened for a 'legitimate' union.

If, whatever you do, it seems inevitable that a union will make some inroads, you should first get any information you can about unions that might be making approaches. Talk to other employers, even talk informally to union officials. If you find a union which, on balance, you prefer, you can use these preliminary informal discussions as a means of laying a foundation for good relationships in the future.

You must avoid having similar groups of employees represented by more than one union. If this happens, inter-union rivalries are almost certain and you, the employer, will suffer.

If a union does recruit members of your staff and approaches you to seek recognition, your answer will depend on the strength of support, assuming you have no objections to this particular union. There is no law which says that you have to recognize a union if it recruits a certain proportion of your staff. As a general rule of thumb, there is not much point in recognizing a union if it represents less than 25 per cent of your staff. If the percentage is between 25 and 50 per cent you will have to consider recognition very carefully, especially if the percentage is growing. In these circumstances, however, you may only need to concede representational rights (see below). You may be hard put to withstand a representation proportion of over 50 per cent, although some employers have.

THE ROLE OF MANAGEMENT

Management typically sees its function as that of directing and control-ling the work force to achieve economic and growth objectives. To this end, it believes that it is the rule-making authority. Management tends to view the enterprise as a unitary system with one source of authority – itself, and one focus of loyalty – the company. It extols the virtue of teamwork, where everyone strives jointly to a common objective, each pulls his weight to the best of his ability, and each accepts his place and his function gladly, following the leadership of the appointed manager or supervisor. These are admirable sentiments but unrealistic, and they sometimes lead to what McClelland has referred to as an 'orgy of avuncular pontification' on the part of the leaders of industry.

The role of management is to exercise authority as well as to build up teamwork, and it is concerned with the development of rules for this purpose; but management has increasingly to accept that it no longer has absolute authority. To a very great extent, management and unions are mutually dependent. For each, the achievement of its own function is dependent upon a working relationship with the other. There are three factors which are important in this relationship.

The first is stability, a firmly established basis for interaction between management and employees. This is why many managers deplore closed shops in theory as an infringement of liberty, but in practice accept that there is less likelihood of trouble if all employees in a job category or unit are members of one union. For the same reason, one union covering all members of the plant may be preferred as a way of reducing the fragmentation of bargaining and of avoiding inter-union rivalries and demarcation – 'who does what' – disputes, even though a monolithic union may be more powerful.

The second factor is trust, a belief that when the bargaining is over and the agreement is reached, both parties will keep their word.

The third factor is understanding of each other's point of view. This does not mean that the parties must always be at one about the fundamental issues that affect them, but they must know how each side sees these issues if a collective agreement is eventually to be negotiated or if a relatively stable working relationship is to be maintained.

THE ROLE OF TRADE UNIONS

The objectives of trade unions can broadly be defined as being:

- To redress the bargaining advantage of the individual workers *vis-à-vis* the individual employer by substituting joint or collective action for individual action.
- To secure improved terms and conditions of employment for their members and the maximum degree of security to enjoy those terms and conditions.
- To obtain improved status for the worker in his work.
- To increase the extent to which unions can exercise democratic control over decisions that affect their interests, by power sharing at the national, corporate and plant level.

Union power is exerted primarily at two levels: at the industry-wide level, to establish joint regulation on basic wages and hours with an employers' association or equivalent; and at the plant level, where the shop stewards' organizations exercise joint control over some aspects of the organization of work and localized terms and conditions of employment. Unions are party to national, local and plant procedure agreements which govern their actions to a greater or lesser extent, depending on their power and on local circumstances.

Unions could be said to be in the business of managing discontent and Clive Jenkins referred to the professional union bargainer as sitting on 'a pinnacle of institutionalized indignation'. But it does not follow that unions introduce conflict; Jenkins also suggested that 'a union official is vocationally a gladiator because the work of the union is basically defensive'.

It can be said that the role of a union is simply to provide a highly organized and continuous form of expression for sectional interests which would exist anyway. Such conflicts of interest are inherent in working relationships and unions can contribute to their solution by bringing issues out into the open and jointly defining with employers procedures for dealing with them.

UNION AGREEMENT

If the union is relatively weak you may only have to concede representational rights. This is a limited form of recognition which simply means that the company accepts the right of a union to represent its members on matters concerning grievances or disciplinary hearings. These representational rights are defined by including in the standard disciplinary and grievance procedures the statement that the employees have the right to be accompanied by a representative who is also an employee of the company.

Representational agreements, however, are not very common, and they are often only a stage towards a full negotiating agreement which conveys to the union the right to negotiate terms and conditions of employment. Such an agreement would include the following statements and provisions.

A statement of intent and common purpose

This will contain words to the effect that: 'The agreement provides a framework which will enable matters of concern to both management and work people to be discussed or negotiated at an appropriate level. The company and the union have a common objective in using the processes of negotiation to achieve results beneficial to both parties. The company recognizes that effective industrial relations are best realized through full representative unions capable of authoritative negotiation. The union for their part recognizes that management has the prime responsibility to manage the undertaking in order to achieve its objectives efficiently.'

Your aim should be to believe in these principles and to make them stick yourself and to persuade your union to make them stick. They should not be allowed to become platitudes. But you have to work at it, and this means continuously establishing and re-establishing them at every contact you have with union representatives, and continually persuading them by the sincerity of what you say and with deeds as well as words that the mutual interests of the company and its employees will be best served by adhering to them.

Representation

A definition is included of the employees represented by the union. Normally these are only union members, but sometimes a union will represent the whole 'bargaining unit', ie all the employees in a company, plant or department, irrespective of whether or not they are union members. A bargaining unit form of representation, where not all employees are union members, has the advantage from the point of view of management that when it comes to ballots on negotiations or industrial action, the non-union members, who are presumably less militant, will be less likely to reject a reasonable offer or to agree to action.

Membership agreement

A membership agreement is a euphemism for a closed shop, if that is accepted by custom and practice or brought in by ballot. A pre-entry closed shop is one in which someone has to be a member of the union before he joins the company. These are to be avoided if possible. A post-entry closed shop is one in which someone is required to become a member of the union after he joins the company, unless he objects to membership on grounds of conscience or other deeply held, genuine personal conviction.

Closed shops come in for a lot of stick from some parts of the media, and they can be oppressive, but many managements like them because they provide for stability in industrial relations. You are much better off if you know where you are with a union; a union which exercises its strength openly and consistently can be managed by being equally strong, open and consistent yourself. Closed shops can help that process. The worst sort of union is the weak one where you never know where you are. Weak shop stewards play into the hands of the militant or subversive elements or abrogate their responsibilities to their full-time officials.

Union facilities

A statement will be made of the facilities granted to unions, including the duties of shop stewards, and the arrangements for union meetings. It is usual to insist on meetings being held outside working hours, although it is often agreed that they can be held on company premises, thus

229

keeping unwanted visitors out. Reference may also be made to the collection of union dues, often through a 'check-off' arrangement for them to be collected by the company, which has the advantage to the company of keeping a tally on the number of union members.

Disputes procedure

The disputes procedure describes a staged method of dealing with an issue from the point when it is first raised on the shop floor until, if not settled earlier, it is referred outside for arbitration or settled in accordance with the agreed procedure for avoiding disputes in the industry. The procedure should provide that, until it is exhausted, no industrial action will be taken by either side.

NEGOTIATING

Negotiating with unions can be a sort of war game in which both sides are pitting their wits against one another and bringing the big guns into play in the shape of sanctions or threats of sanctions to get what they want. There are some conventions which help to determine how negotiations take place, and the 'going rate' will affect the level of settlements, but power politics and the respective strengths of will of the two sides will also be important factors.

Negotiating conventions

The conventions usually accepted by responsible trade unions and management are:

1. Whatever happens during the bargaining, both parties are using the bargaining process in the hope of coming to a settlement.
2. Attacks, hard words, threats and (controlled) losses of temper are perfectly legitimate tactics to underline determination to get one's way and to shake the opponent's confidence and self-possession. These are treated by both sides as legitimate tactics and should not be allowed to shake the basic belief in each other's integrity or desire to settle without taking drastic action.
3. Off-the-record discussions are mutually beneficial as a means of probing attitudes and intentions and smoothing the way to a settlement; but they should not be referred to specifically in formal bargaining sessions unless both sides agree in advance.
4. Each side should normally be prepared to move from its original position.

5. It is normal, although not inevitable, for the negotiation to proceed by alternate offers and counter-offers from each side which lead steadily towards a settlement.
6. Concessions, once made, cannot be withdrawn.
7. Firm offers must not be withdrawn, although it is legitimate to make and withdraw conditional offers.
8. Third parties should not be brought in until both parties are agreed that no further progress would be made without them.
9. The final agreement should mean exactly what it says. There should be no trickery, and the terms agreed should be implemented without amendment.
10. If possible, the final settlement should be framed in such a way as to reduce the extent to which the opponent obviously loses face or credibility.

Negotiating techniques and tactics

The following are the techniques and tactics you should use when negotiating:

1. *Prepare for the negotiation* by defining the maximum you would want to concede and an opening offer which will leave you enough room for manoeuvre in reaching your target. At the same time assess what the union is likely to ask for and to expect. Prepare also your replies to the points the union representatives are likely to make. These may include the contention that company pay levels or other terms and conditions of employment are below the going rate and/ or they may refer to the level of settlements elsewhere, the rate of inflation, productivity improvements and the ability of the company to pay.
2. *Opening tactics*: these should be to:
   - open realistically and move moderately;
   - challenge your opponent's position as it stands; do not destroy his ability to move;
   - explore attitudes, ask questions, observe behaviour and, above all, listen in order to assess your opponent's strengths and weaknesses, his tactics and the extent to which he may be bluffing;
   - make no concessions of any kind at this stage;
   - be non-committal about proposals and explanations (do not talk too much).
3. *Bargaining*: after the opening moves you begin the main bargaining phase during which you narrow the gap between the initial

positions and try to persuade your opponent that your case is sufficiently strong to force him to close at a less advantageous point than he had planned. Your tactics should be to:

- always make conditional proposals: 'If you will do this, I will consider doing that';
- don't make one-sided concessions; wherever possible, trade off against a concession from the other party: 'If I concede x then I expect you to concede y';
- negotiate on the whole package; do not allow your opponent to pick you off item by item, and keep the issues open to extract the maximum benefit from your potential trade-offs.

4. *Closing*: when and how you close is a matter of judgement, and depends on your assessment of the strength of your opponent's case and his determination to see it through. The closing techniques available are:

- making a concession from the package, preferably a minor one which is traded off against an agreement to settle. The concession can be offered more positively than in the bargaining stage: 'If you will agree to settle x, I will concede y';
- doing a deal; splitting the difference, or bringing in something new, such as extending the settlement timescale, agreeing to make back-payments, phasing increases, making a joint declaration of intent to do something in the future (eg introducing a productivity plan);
- summarizing what has happened to date, emphasizing the concessions that have been made and the extent to which you have moved, and stating that you have reached your final position;
- applying pressure through a threat of the dire consequences that will follow if your offer is not accepted;
- giving your opponent a choice between two courses of action.

Do not make a final offer unless you mean it. If it is not really your final offer and your opponent calls your bluff, you will have to make further concessions and your credibility will be undermined. He will, of course, attempt to force you into revealing the extent to which you have reached your final position. Do not allow him to hurry you. If you want to avoid committing yourself and thus devaluing the word 'final', state as positively as you can that this is as far as you are prepared to go leaving the words 'at this stage' unspoken.

PARTICIPATION

Participation is the most positive approach to dealing with employees collectively. Union negotiations are too often fire-fighting affairs – fundamentally unconstructive.

Definition and aims

Participation is the joint involvement of management and employees in making decisions on matters of mutual concern. These decisions can be restricted to amenities such as working conditions and canteens, but they are most fruitful if they go more deeply into management affairs, especially those concerned with productivity and quality.

The benefits of participation, as defined by the Industrial Participation Association, are that:

1. It is both reasonable and just that the employees of a company should have the means to influence the major decisions that affect their working lives.
2. Its essential purpose must be to improve the efficiency and productivity of the enterprise, by enabling employees at all levels to make a more effective contribution.

Types of participation

The main types of participation are:

1. Ad hoc *working parties or project teams* to deal with a specific problem – this is often the best way.
2. *Team briefing (briefing groups)*, as described in Chapter 7, which provide a means of two-way communication.
3. *Joint consultative committees* which meet formally and sometimes, but not always, involve union representatives (some unions see joint consultation as a divisive tactic of management aimed to reduce their influence – which of course it often is).
4. *Quality circles*: these are groups of employees led by their supervisor who meet voluntarily to discuss and resolve quality problems or to achieve some other important target. The members are trained in problem-solving techniques and the sequence of events in a typical quality circle is as follows:
   - the members identify problems in their work area, although, on occasion, supervisors or managers can indicate problems that need to be solved;
   - when the problem has been identified the circle agrees a realistic

233

goal for its activities, such as to reduce defects from 6 to 3 per cent over a period of three months;

- the circle draws up a plan for solving the problem using appropriate analytical techniques;
- the base data are collected by members of the circle and possible solutions to the problem are reviewed. Expertise from supervision or technical personnel can be called on;
- when a solution has been agreed the circle presents to management its analysis of the problem and its proposals for solving it;
- the circle is responsible for implementing solutions agreed by management. It monitors results, carries out tests as necessary and reports on progress.

Requirements for successful participation

The ten basic requirements for successful participation are:

1. The objectives of participation must be defined, discussed and agreed by all concerned.
2. The objectives must be related to tangible and significant aspects of the job, the process of management or the formulation of policies that affect the interests of employees. They must not relate to peripheral matters such as welfare or social amenities, ie in Herzberg's phrase, they should not be concerned with the 'hygiene' factors alone.
3. Management must believe and must be seen to believe in participation. Actions speak better than words and management must demonstrate that it will put into effect the joint decisions made during discussions.
4. The unions must believe in participation as a genuine means of advancing the interests of their members and not simply as a way of getting more power. They should show by their actions that they are prepared to support unpopular decisions to which they have been a party.
5. Joint consultation machinery should be in line with any existing systems of negotiation and representation. It should not be supported by management as a possible way of reducing the powers of the union. If this naive approach is taken it will fail – it always does. Joint consultation should be regarded as a complementary process of integrative bargaining to the distributive bargaining that takes place in negotiating committees. A separate consultative system may not be necessary in a well-organized 100 per cent union establishment.

6. If management does introduce joint consultation as a means of keeping unions out, it should be prepared to widen the terms of reference as much as possible to cover issues which might normally be the subject of negotiation with unions. This approach can backfire if the staff representatives acquire a taste for negotiation and turn to the unions if they find they are not getting what they want.

7. Joint consultative committees should relate to a defined working unit, should never meet unless there is something specific to discuss, and should always conclude their meetings with agreed points which are implemented quickly.

8. Employee and management representatives should be properly briefed and trained and have all the information they require.

9. Managers and supervisors should be kept in the picture.

10. Consultation should take place before decisions are made.

PART VI

Human Resource Utilization

Introduction

Human resource management is concerned as much with improving productivity – the utilization of human resources – as with any of its other elements (obtaining, developing, rewarding, motivating and managing the members of the organization). This is recognized in the code of practice of the British Institute of Personnel Management which states that 'personnel practitioners who are IPM members provide professional knowledge, advice and support to their employers on the most effective use of the human resource'.

Productivity management is a continuing and demanding responsibility. Too often it has been relegated to under-resourced organization and methods of work study departments. How often does productivity appear on the agenda of a typical board meeting or as a significant part of a corporate plan? In many organizations it hardly ever gets discussed at this level unless it is a crude drive to reduce overheads without looking at more positive approaches to increasing output.

Human resource utilization is dealt with in the final part of this book not as an afterthought but rather as the culminating point in the range of HRM programmes which an organization needs to achieve its objectives of increased growth and prosperity in the private sector, and better levels of service and efficiency in the public sector.

16. Employing People Productively

THE NEED FOR ACTION

The costs of employing your human resources may amount to as much as 50 per cent of your turnover, if your company is labour-intensive. Even though it may drop to 10 to 20 per cent in a capital-intensive industry, this may still be a significant factor in determining the profitability of your firm or the ability of a public service to fulfil its function economically.

Productivity, as measured by wage cost per unit of output and payroll costs as a percentage of turnover, is therefore the key factor in measuring the effectiveness of human resources in an organization. Work measurement programmes often reveal that, when the performance of staff not on an incentive scheme is rated, the result is no more than 50 to 60 per cent of the standard that can be expected from an average worker. Productivity audits of manufacturing and distribution activities consistently pinpoint opportunities for improving output by from 25 to 40 per cent with much the same plant and human resources. Similarly, clerical work measurement programmes frequently save more than 15 per cent of staff without affecting output or quality.

It is remarkable that when firms have to cut back staff because of falling orders they frequently reduce numbers by a far greater proportion than the decline in activity levels without affecting throughput.

The scope for improvement is tremendous and so are the pay-offs, as the analysis from company reports as Table 16.1 shows.

Payroll as % of sales	Percentage increase in profit before tax* from improvement in productivity of:			
	5%	*10%*	*20%*	*40%*
20	20	40	80	160
30	30	60	120	240
40	40	80	160	320
50	50	100	200	500

*Assumes a return on sales of 5 per cent

Table 16.1 *Potential impact of greater productivity on profits*

WHAT CAN YOU DO?

The first thing to do is to overcome apathy. Both managers and members of the work force must be persuaded somehow that they have a common interest in increasing output per head. This is not an easy exercise. It requires considerable powers of leadership from the top and a continuing campaign for getting across the need to do something about productivity. It means positive programmes for motivating and involving all concerned to obtain their commitment to improvement.

The following actions are required to improve the use of your human resources:

1. Conduct a productivity audit.
2. Improve manpower budgeting and control techniques.
3. Initiate a method improvement programme.
4. Introduce work measurement.
5. Use payment by results, bonus and profit sharing schemes where you are certain that they will improve productivity.
6. Improve motivation.
7. Involve your employees in seeking improved methods.
8. Introduce new technology.
9. Negotiate productivity agreements where appropriate.
10. Introduce training programmes based on an analysis of productivity training needs.

Each of these actions is discussed below.

Productivity audit

A productivity audit starts by measuring what is happening and continues to look at each aspect of using human resources.

Measurement
Productivity can be measured as a series of ratios:

$$\frac{\text{output obtained}}{\text{input expected}} = \frac{\text{performance achieved}}{\text{resources concerned}} = \frac{\text{effectiveness}}{\text{efficiency}}$$

High productivity reflects the full (ie effective and efficient) use of human resources. It is related to two variables:

1. *Input variables* will include payroll costs, the associated costs of employment, the number of people employed and the number of hours worked or time taken.
2. *Output variables* will include units produced, products sold, tasks completed, revenues obtained, value added, responsibilities met and standards reached (including standard hours produced).

A wide variety of productivity ratios can be derived from these input and output variables and these can be analysed and added to under the following headings:

1. *Output ratios*
   - $\dfrac{\text{units produced or processed}}{\text{number of employees}}$
   - $\dfrac{\text{sales turnover}}{\text{number of employees}}$
   - $\dfrac{\text{added value}}{\text{number of employees}}$
   - $\dfrac{\text{standard hours produced}}{\text{number of employees}}$
2. *Cost ratios*
   - $\dfrac{\text{wages cost}}{\text{units produced}}$
   - $\dfrac{\text{sales turnover}}{\text{payroll/employment costs}}$
   - $\dfrac{\text{added value}}{\text{payroll/employment costs}}$
   - $\dfrac{\text{actual labour cost per standard hour}}{\text{target cost per standard hour}}$
   - $\dfrac{\text{standard hours produced}}{\text{labour costs}}$
3. *Performance ratios*
   - $\dfrac{\text{standard hours produced}}{\text{actual hours worked}}$
   - $\dfrac{\text{actual performance}}{\text{target performance}}$

The choice is ample and you should select one or more to suit your own circumstances. There are very few occasions, however, when the basic index of

$$\frac{\text{results}}{\text{resources}} \quad \text{ie} \quad \frac{\text{sales}}{\text{employees}}$$

will not prove to be the most useful of all.

The audit

The audit should start by looking at the relevant output, cost and performance ratios. Trends should be studied and comparisons made wherever possible between the ratios achieved in different parts of the enterprise and with other comparable organizations. The reasons for positive or adverse trends or comparisons should be examined so that you can decide what actions can be taken to exploit good results or to correct weaknesses or declines in productivity.

The audit should examine specifically in the light of these comparisons:

1. *Human resource budgets*: to ensure that they set suitable and realistic productivity targets.
2. *Human resource control systems*: to ensure that departmental and individual performance standards are set and monitored and that corrective action is taken when necessary.
3. *Work methods*: to ensure that a continuous programme of reviewing and improving them is taking place in all parts of the organization.
4. *Work measurement*: to ensure that it is used wherever possible to develop standards, give better control information, improve methods and produce effective incentive schemes.
5. *Payment methods*: to ensure that the maximum use is made of incentive schemes and that pay increases are related to properly assessed and measured improvements in performance.
6. *Motivation*: to ensure that methods of management and supervision and conditions of employment encourage positive motivation.
7. *Involvement*: to ensure that employees are involved in seeking ways of improving productivity and appreciate that improvements in productivity benefit themselves as well as the company.
8. *Training*: to ensure that training programmes are geared to improving efficiency, effectiveness and, therefore, productivity.
9. *Technology*: to ensure that the scope for labour saving by

introducing new technology and mechanization is fully explored and acted upon.

10. *Productivity agreements*: to explore the possibility of negotiating productivity agreements.

Human resource budgeting and control

The budget
Human resource budgeting was described in detail in Chapter 8. In essence, it should start from forecasts of activity levels, and guidelines should be given in the shape of target ratios, for example:

- Employment costs to sales turnover.
- Turnover of sales value of production per employee.
- Indirects to directs.

Other targets can be given as necessary, for example:

- Reduce number of indirects by x per cent.
- Hold any increase in numbers to at least y per cent less than the forecast increase in activity levels.
- Reduce percentage of employment cost overheads to sales turnover by z per cent.

The number of people required should be estimated by using the human resource planning techniques of ratio analysis, work measurement and econometric models described in Chapter 8.

Control
If you want to control employment costs you need to:

1. *Plan* what you aim to achieve. This means setting employment and productivity/performance targets and standards and ensuring that everyone understands and accepts them.
2. *Measure* regularly what has been achieved.
3. *Compare* actual achievements with the plan.
4. *Take action* to correct deviations from the plan.

Method improvement

Method improvement covers all aspects of rationalization, work simplification, value engineering and office management designed to reduce manufacturing and processing costs. It is based on method study, which is defined as the systematic recording and critical examination of existing and proposed ways of doing work as a means of developing and applying easier and more effective methods and reducing costs. The outcome of a method study should be less costly, quicker and more efficient methods achieved by:

- *Work simplification*: eliminating unnecessary operations, movements and paperwork.
- *Mechanization*: introducing new tools or equipment to speed up processing.
- *Automation*: replacing human labour with machines or electronic equipment.
- *Facilities improvement*: providing more efficient services, improving the availability of materials, parts and tools, improving the working environment through better layouts and ergonomic studies.
- *Better planning and scheduling* of work.

Method study techniques
A method study investigation consists of the following stages:

1. *Select* the work to be studied, which means identifying suitable projects where there are likely to be significant benefits, setting objectives and terms of reference and drawing up a programme.
2. *Record* all the relevant facts – the work carried out and the sequence of activities or steps of a process.
3. *Examine* the facts critically by asking these questions:
   - what is done? why do it?
   - how is it done? why do it that way?
   - where is it done? why do it there?
   - when is it done? why do it then?
   - who does it? why that person?
4. *Develop* the new method, going carefully into both the costs and benefits and evaluating alternatives systematically.
5. *Install* the method as a standard practice.
6. *Maintain* the standard practice.

Work measurement

Definition and aims
Work measurement is the application of techniques designed to establish the work content of a specified task and the time for a qualified worker to carry out that job at a defined level of performance. The aims of work measurement are to:

246

1. *Determine current manning levels*: by objectively providing an indication of 'should take' time, work measurement gives management the ability to compare the amount of time actually spent with the amount of time that should have been spent. When current manpower levels are in excess of what time standards show to be required, reductions in the numbers employed can be achieved. When the reverse applies, the current level can be increased.
2. *Determine future human resource needs*: by defining the time required to perform specific tasks, work measurement makes it possible to translate forecast activity levels into anticipated staff requirements.
3. *Monitor performance*: by providing the common denominator of standard hours, work measurement enables the performance of different units to be compared. Actuals can be compared with targets to indicate where corrective action may be required.
4. *Assist in budget preparation*: the time standards can be used to convert forecast volumes into the total number of hours required, which can in turn be converted by the application of hourly rates into the cost of labour.
5. *Provide the basis for incentive schemes* which relate pay to performance as measured by the ratio between standard and actual hours.

Overall, therefore, work measurement provides an analytical basis for budgeting and controlling human resource costs. It can be an important aid to increasing productivity by providing standards against which performance can be planned, monitored and improved.

Work measurement techniques
Work measurement techniques can roughly be divided into two categories:

1. Those that measure the time that should be taken, using time study, synthesis or predetermined motion time systems (PMTS), or analytical estimating.
2. Those that measure the time that is being taken using self-recording systems, activity or work sampling and batch control or short interval scheduling.

Wherever possible, a technique which produces 'should take' standard times is to be preferred. This gives a target level of performance based on an analysis of work that can be done by experienced workers and provides a much better basis for budgeting and control and for incentive schemes.
    A technique based on 'is being taken' times is less desirable because it

may perpetuate existing malpractices; but it at least gives some indication of standard times, which can be used for estimating staff requirements more scientifically than the usual guess-work methods. Activity sampling is the best approach, followed by batch control in suitable circumstances. Self-recording is better than nothing, but should only be used as a last resort.

Payment by results schemes

Paying for productivity means that you should use incentive schemes wherever possible, or at least establish some objective criteria for relating pay to performance. People want money and will work harder and better to get more of it. It is not the only method of motivation but it is one of the most important.

Incentive schemes as described in Chapter 11 are usually most suitable for manual workers. Pure payment by results schemes are much more difficult to operate for white collar staff, except for those in selling jobs. It is still possible, however, to provide rewards for such staff which are related to company results (profit sharing) or individual performance (results-oriented assessment schemes as described in Chapter 7, or bonus schemes as dealt with in Chapter 8).

Improve motivation

Pay will motivate people, but there are other important motivating factors, as discussed in Chapter 5. The main motivating techniques you should develop systematically in your organization are:

1. Job enrichment (Chapter 3).
2. Better leadership (Chapter 6).
3. Ensuring that you get your message across about the need for higher productivity *and* how it benefits individual employees as well (Chapter 7).

Involvement

Involvement is important: people will be better motivated if they participate in productivity improvement programmes, and they are more likely to accept the results of the programmes if they are associated with the studies and investigations leading to proposals for change. Further identification will be achieved if they participate in implementing change, and steps are taken to mitigate fears about redundancies and to point out how the company and the people concerned will both benefit.

Involvement is, however, easier to propose than to achieve. Many organizations have successfully used quality circles (as discussed in Chapter 11) to obtain improvements, but they take a lot of time and trouble to introduce and manage.

Involvement should also be looked for on an individual basis. If people feel that their job is worthwhile they are more likely to look for ways of improving their performance. Giving them more responsibility through better job design (see Chapter 3) is a good way of doing this.

Training

Productivity is dependent on the skill, attitude and application of those carrying out the work. Getting people to adopt the right attitude to work and to work harder is largely a matter of motivation, pay and the way in which they are managed. But skill and, to a certain degree, attitudes can be developed by training.

Training using the techniques described in Chapter 13 should play a prominent part in your productivity improvement programme. Its purpose is not simply to show people how to do a job and then let them pick up for themselves the required standards of output. Training should extend to the point at which trainees reach a level of output and quality equivalent to that maintained by the experienced worker who is achieving the targets and standards expected of him.

Another important aim of productivity training is to enable the organization and the individual to make the best use of the skills the latter possesses. Under-utilization of the skills available is one of the most common reasons for low productivity. Training can bring out latent abilities. It can also develop attitudes to work which help people to appreciate the importance of better productivity, to themselves as well as to the company.

New technology

Productivity is, obviously, not only a matter of human skill and effort but is also dependent upon the aids to more efficient performance available in the shape of information technology, mechanization and automation. It is beyond the scope of this book to discuss these approaches. But you need constantly to bear in mind, when introducing new technology, that its effectiveness will depend entirely on the skill and motivation of those operating it. Training in the new skills required is therefore vital, and so is involvement in planning for and implementing change.

Productivity agreements

A productivity agreement can be defined as one in which workers agree to make a change, or a number of changes, in working practice that will lead to a higher level of pay or other benefits. Productivity bargaining produces a 'package deal' covering a number of issues. The different parties make concessions on particular aspects in order to achieve an agreement considered to be of overall advantage to all concerned. The main characteristics of a productivity agreement are:

1. It is usually related to one plant and covers all the manual employees in that plant.
2. It records agreement on the means by which improved efficiency is to be achieved, eg through greater labour flexibility by the relaxation of demarcation rules, reducing unnecessary overtime, relaxing restrictions on output.
3. It incorporates either: 1) buying out on the basis of a quid pro quo, offering immediate wage increases in exchange for concessions such as the relaxation of rigid demarcation rules, elimination of some breaks, forfeiture of craftsmen's 'mates', reduction in the total labour force; or 2) an agreement for allowing savings to be accumulated over a period of say, six to 12 months, when they are then split on a 50:50, or some proportionate basis between workers and the company. A higher proportion would go to employees in a labour-intensive concern than in a capital-intensive company. The savings may be worked out as in the Scanlon scheme, by computing the savings in labour costs resulting from a reduction in the ratio of labour costs to sales value or added value.
4. It may provide for the introduction of a new job-evaluated pay structure or a new payment system such as the replacement of piece work by measured day work.

Conditions for productivity bargaining
To be effective, productivity bargaining requires:

- Total commitment on the part of senior management.
- A comprehensive approach to cost reduction and to the distribution of savings from cost reduction.
- A supportive climate of opinion throughout the organization.
- An agreed basis for measuring improvements in productivity.
- A more sophisticated approach by management to the communication of information about performance to the trade union.

Productivity bargaining steps
The main steps in productivity bargaining are:

1. Analyse the productivity audit to identify areas where improvements in productivity achieved by the removal of restrictive or wasteful practices, or by other means, could result from a productivity agreement. The restrictive and wasteful practices could include such items as:
   - restrictions on the flexible use of labour;
   - restrictions on the use of labour-saving machinery or plant;
   - overmanning;
   - uneconomic rules for overtime;
   - restrictions on recruitment or training;
   - excessive tea or meal break allowances at the beginning or end of shifts;
   - restrictions on the use of work measurement;
   - over-rigid or lengthy procedures for dealing with grievances;
2. Set up a joint working party with the trade union to agree on the approach to be used in negotiating a productivity agreement. This working party would assess the scope for jointly agreeing ways of improving productivity as a means of financing higher pay scales or providing greater security of employment.
3. Conduct a detailed joint study into the productivity problems of the company to agree on causes and identify remedies which could be incorporated in the productivity deal. This study should calculate the cost savings and other benefits that could be obtained. The aim should be to make the agreement self-financing, ie pay increases are covered by cost savings or extra revenue.
4. Conduct the negotiations with the aims of agreeing:
   - any changes in manning levels or working practices that will contribute to increased productivity;
   - the cost savings or increased earnings that will result from the changes;
   - the way in which payments for productivity will be distributed to employees.
5. Communicate the agreement to all concerned, setting out the changes in working practices and the payments to be made in return.
6. Prepare an implementation programme in consultation with the union and ensure that the programme is carefully monitored.

Benefits of productivity agreements
Productivity agreements can bring measurable benefits by removing

restrictive practices and eliminating traditional and now outdated manning levels. The joint approach can be used to gain more commitment to introducing change. Everyone is involved and this produces greater productivity consciousness throughout the organization, among management as well as employees.

The benefits can only be achieved after the hard work required to obtain the facts and negotiate the deal. Trade unions will not give anything away, even in hard times, and you must be prepared for some tough negotiating sessions, but the effort can be worthwhile.

CONCLUSION

Human resource management means getting the organization right, providing effective motivation and leadership, obtaining and developing the right people, paying and treating them fairly, and getting them involved in working productively. The following is a case study showing how a company successfully changed its way of organizing, managing and motivating its work force.

Case study

How to Avoid the British Disease
The low productivity which dogs British industry can be explained in many ways. One reason could be the class antagonisms that perpetuate the gap between management and men and make it almost impossible to achieve a sense of common purpose.

Allen Chatterton and Ray Leonard in *How to Avoid the British Disease* explained how the problem was tackled at Long and Crawford Ltd, a Manchester-based engineering firm of which Allen Chatterton is works director and where, despite a recession in the industry, order books are bulging. Mr Chatterton, encouraged by his managing director, Ken Buckley, has, over a period of ten years, tried to develop a co-operative relationship with the work force. His aim was to eliminate the class differences which, as in so many industries, were seen to be hampering production.

At the start of the programme, management and the work force were barely talking to each other; niggling disputes cropped up frequently with the inevitable result of low sales and a dismal return on capital. Morale was low, labour turnover high and the payment system had virtually broken down. Everyone was worse off.

The chief executive and the board started to ask themselves simple questions. Is the form of organization to blame? What are the work force reacting to, or against? Would a better approach make people work better? As a result of a careful appraisal, backed by a survey of shop floor attitudes, a number of reforms were gradually introduced. At one level they read like clichés falling out of a management manual – job enrichment, incentives, involvement – but cumulatively they added up to something of a revolution.

First, according to Mr Chatterton, the company has adopted a community style of management which concentrates on the natural groups that form in the working population, including the identification of natural group leaders. A fortnightly meeting is held with shop stewards, even if there is nothing on the agenda, and stewards are encouraged to go on day-release courses to learn about the financial side of running a business.

Second, if there is a problem, say of a technical nature, all of the people involved are brought together to talk it through with the objective of harnessing a wide spread of expertise to solve the problem, rather than trying to identify who was responsible.

Third, the company has tried to improve communications by flattening out the management structure from seven layers to five: managing director, works directors, works managers, foremen and the shop floor.

Staff have been given the freedom to go across the strata: the purchasing side can move 'horizontally' to talk to sales without first having to go 'vertically' through their own superiors in purchasing and up one hierarchical tree in order to go down another. Anyone can stop the works director to discuss a problem, and decisions are not made without the foreman being involved.

Fourth, job enrichment is pursued by trying to allow the work force to control, as far as practicable, the rhythms and structure of their working environment. Assembly lines have been reorganized in accordance with ideas put forward by the work force who, for example, elected to work with a 'family' of machines (eg lathes), where they could retain their established working groups rather than mixing together milling machines and lathes under the same foreman.

On the assembly line, one man now completely assembles a piece of switchgear from the first to the final stage instead of being a cog on the assembly line.

The company is also working towards a harmonization of practices such as sick pay and pension schemes for the shop floor, and time off for visits to hospital and the dentist. Lateness penalties for the shop floor are being greatly reduced.

Behind all these reforms there is the dynamo of an incentive scheme. Roughly one-third of earnings spring from a payment by results system, based on a price per piece for work submitted at the end of the week. But even here the workers can opt either to work individually or collectively on payment by results. There is also provision within working groups either to work at a more tranquil pace, which older workers prefer, or flat out, which younger men with families tend to prefer.

Mr Chatterton sees his job as trying to get people to identify with the company by setting up a community spirit. This does not make the factory a paradise to work in, but it has clearly reduced many of the tensions apparent in most factories and has resulted in gains for both the company and the work force.

Index

criteria for success, 66, 79–80,
181–182
for sales staff, 183–184
incremental scales, 179
Industrial Society, 110
information technology, 12, 39
initiating structure, 93
Institute of Personnel Management,
239
integration, 1, 3, 56–57
intelligence tests, 160–161
internal advertisements, 147
International Telephone &
Telegraph Company, 34
interviewing, counselling, 218–19
interviewing, employment, 154–159
basic approach, 156
plan, 156
purpose of, 155
techniques, 157–158
involvement, 3, 28, 248–249

Job analysis, 141–142, 174, 201
job applications, sifting of, 153–154
job classification, 175, 176
job descriptions, 142–144
job design, 43–44, 81, 249
job enrichment, 44–45, 81
job evaluation,
aims of, 173–174
factors, 174
programme, 176–177
job evaluation schemes, 175–176
job instruction, 204
job satisfaction, 69, 73
job specification see personnel
specification
joint consultation, 225, 234, 235
joint consultative committees, 113,
233, 235

KITA, 71, 72

Labour wastage, 120–121
law of the situation, 95–96
leader, the, 4, 12, 28, 84–86, 87
authority of, 91–92

demands on, 90–91
how leaders do it, 92–94
types of, 87–88
what leaders do, 89
leadership, 12, 28, 37, 81
contingency theory of, 96
definition, 83
factors influencing success, 86
objectives of, 83–84
qualities of, 85–86
roles, 90
situational, 98, 99–100
skills, 98–101
leadership styles, 96–98, 100
learning theory, 199–200
lecturing, 205–207
line and staff organization, 46
London Life, 26

Management of change, 36–37,
59–60
management by objectives, 13–14,
24
management by walking around
(MBWA), 31
management development,
aims, 208
methods, 208–211
planned experience, 211–212
management inventory, 204–211
management, role of, 226–227
management style, 23, 30, 37
analysis of, 22
Blake's grid, 93–94
definition, 17
leadership styles, 96–98, 100
management training, 212
managerial behaviour, 1
manpower planning see human
resource planning
market rates, 170–171, 175
matrix organization, 46, 48
Matsushita company, 21
mentors, 212
method improvement, 245–246
method study, 246
money and motivation, 78–79

Index of Authors Cited